Old King Cole

A MUSICAL PLAY IN TWO ACTS

Book and Lyrics by
Joe Grenzeback

Music by
Haakon Bergh

Samuel French, Inc.

PRICE, 75 CENTS

ANNE OF GREEN GABLES

Comedy. 3 acts. By Alice Chadwicke. 4 males, 10 females. Interior. Modern costumes.

L. M. Montgomery's famous and beloved best-seller has now been converted into a magically beautiful and touching play. Green Gables is the home of lovable Matthew Cuthbert and his stern sister, Marilla, who has never been known to thaw out. When they agree to adopt a boy to help with the farm work, imagine their consternation when Anne Shirley, a girl in her teens, is sent by the orphanage by mistake! Anne, with her vivid imagination, her charitable viewpoint, touches Matthew's heart, but it takes time to reach the soft and tender heart beneath Marilla's hard exterior. The comedy that ensues through Anne's many unfortunate mistakes caused by her all too vivid imagination, her loyalty to Matthew and Marilla, her attachment for her bosom friend, Diana Barry, her feud with Gilbert Blythe, the wealthiest boy in town, the episode of Marilla's old amethyst brooch, and many more heart-warming incidents are finally woven into this play. Anne is the sort of part that every young girl will adore playing. The play breathes of youth, is thoroughly modern in spirit, very simple to prepare and present.

(Royalty, $25.00.)

TISH

Comedy. 3 acts. By Alice Chadwicke. 5 males, 8 females. Interior. Modern costumes.

Here are Mary Roberts Rinehart's most famous stories made into an hilarious play. Tish is a middle-aged spinster; blunt, outspoken, and entirely lovable. Tish, with Lizzie and Aggie, her two boon companions, starts on a motor tour in the southwest. It ends somewhat abruptly when Tish drives the car through Luther Hopkins's plate glass window. This little incident starts a series of mad accidents through which Tish sails with flying colors. She tries to recover the money stolen from the hotel. She is mistaken for an international female spy. Whether she is trying to help Aggie recover her lost teeth or straighten out the tangled romances of the young couples Tish is on the spot getting people out of one difficulty and into another. Tish as a character and a play will delight your audiences.

(Royalty, $25.00.)

Old King Cole

A MUSICAL PLAY IN TWO ACTS

Book and Lyrics by
Joe Grenzeback

Music by
Haakon Bergh

SAMUEL FRENCH, INC.

25 WEST 45TH STREET   NEW YORK 36

7623 SUNSET BOULEVARD   HOLLYWOOD 46

LONDON   TORONTO

OLD KING COLE

OLD KING COLE

STORY OF THE PLAY

In preparation for his daughter's coming-out party, King Cole calls his fiddlers to a rehearsal—only to discover that the Royal Fiddles have disappeared. It develops that Crunch, the Royal Fiddle Polisher, has faddled the fiddles in an attempt to prove himself a great magician. Moreover, he tells a lie. As punishment, he is banished from the kingdom. The fiddles are replaced.

To revenge himself upon the King, Crunch leaves behind a magic box. Whatever is placed in the box cannot be taken out except by virtue of a magic song known only to Crunch. Unaware of this condition, King Cole allows the new fiddles to be put into the box for safe-keeping. Once inside, they stick fast—and in the process of trying to release them, the sunlight itself is trapped inside the box!

Despite the King's offer of "his heart's desire" to anyone who can break the magic spell, all efforts fail. In time, Crunch returns and offers to release the sunlight and the fiddles in exchange for a crown. The bargain is made—but Crunch has forgotten the magic song! The Apprentice Jester, one Nicholas of Nowhere, finds a clue to the elusive song and all is made right again.

OLD KING COLE

CHARACTERS

(In the order of their appearance)

(9 males; 7 females)

TIC, *a Royal Fiddler.*
TAC, *another.*
TOE, *another.*
MRS. SMEDLY, *the Royal Castlekeeper.*
AMELIA, *a Lady-in-Waiting.*
CELIA, *another.*
ARABELLA, *another.*
QUEEN, *of the Kingdom of Haw.*
GROG, *Prime Minister and several other things, also of Haw.*
KING COLE *of Haw. A merry old soul.*
NICK, *a newcomer.*
CRUNCH, *the Royal Fiddle-Polisher.*
PENELOPE, *the Princess.*
BLACK SMITH, *a blacksmith.*
LOCK SMITH, *his wife, a locksmith.*
MESSENGER, *from the edge of the Kingdom.*

THE TIME

A month or so before the Party.

THE PLACE

The action of the play takes place in the throne-room of King Cole's Castle:

ACT ONE
    SCENE 1: *Morning.*
    SCENE 2: *Later the same day.*
ACT TWO
    A few weeks later.

CHARACTER DESCRIPTIONS AND COSTUMES

Tic, Tac, Toe: *The Royal Fiddlers. They are essentially interchangeable: three peas from the same pod. They share a great eagerness of manner, which is reflected in their movements. They are any age short of senility.*
Costume: Basically tights with a brightly colored three-quarter length over-garment: a stylized sort of Royal livery.

Mrs. Smedly: *The Royal Castlekeeper. A dignified, almost prim woman: the perennial maiden aunt. She is perhaps 50.*
Costume: Her gown is simple and relatively austere; floor-length and high at the neck.

Amelia, Celia, Arabella: *The Ladies-in-Waiting. Vivacious and attractive, but with a disconcerting tendency to giggle. They are 16 to 18: old enough to be adult, but young enough not to insist upon it.*
Costume: Identical as to style and pattern, but with individual variations in color. Long skirts and laced bodices; small, uniform caps, preferably starched.

Queen: *A warm, sensible person, but inclined to worry. She is everyone's mother, but only old enough to be Penelope's: under 40, but not much.*
Costume: Crown, gown and usual trimmings.

Grog: *A man with many jobs, he has need of much energy. As a result, he is forever running on—both verbally and physically. He is tremendously conscientious and proud of it. He might be 45.*
Costume: In general, his many-pocketed clothes resemble a magician's robes (circa Merlin, et. al.). He is hung, strung and stuffed with the impedimenta of his various offices. His high-crowned, flat-topped hat

5

*contains a cloth extension which, when pulled out
at the top, converts the headpiece to a Jester's cap,
bells and all.*

KING COLE: *A merry old soul and rather portly. He is a
bouncy little man who tends to chuckle his words
when he talks and to have a direct, good-natured and
somewhat naive reaction to almost everything. He is
essentially ageless.*

*Costume: Crown and robes, preferably in bright,
warm colors: yellows and reds.*

NICK: *A well-behaved but rather cocky lad of perhaps 17.
He takes things as they come, but has an eye for the
niceties. In another sort of story, he would be the
Good Prince.*

*Costume: Tights and jerkin, with a Robin Hood style
cap trimmed with a small chicken feather.*

CRUNCH: *The Royal Fiddle-Polisher. A small, grumbly
sort of man who is no better than he should be. Bad
enough at times, he is most reminiscent of a petulant
child. He is 20 or 30 or somewhere in between.*

*Costume: Tights, with an awkward, straight-hanging
over-garment. The general effect is ragged as well as
comic. In Act One, he wears a tall, pointed hat, similar to a dunce-cap. In Act Two, he wears a low,
broadbrimmed hat, an over-sized cloak, and a long
muffler.*

PENELOPE: *A bright, pretty girl, as every Princess should
be. She is 16, and except for the fact that she giggles
less and tends to be more thoughtful, she is very
much like the Ladies-in-Waiting.*

*Costume: Very similar to the Ladies-in-Waiting, but
distinctive in terms of color and detail. If anything,
her costume should be more simple than theirs, well-
fashioned and neat. She wears no head-gear except
as the action demands that she put on her crown.
(See Prop List.)*

BLACK SMITH: *A small, wiry man, proud of his trade and
sure of his personal proficiency in it. His stance and
manners are those of the smithy. About 25.*

Costume: Jerkin and knee-britches, with a belt that

serves primarily to support his tool pouch. He may or may not wear a hat or "stocking" cap.

LOCK SMITH: *A large woman with a voice to match. She towers over her husband, but seems oblivious to the fact. One suspects that she is a handy person with an anvil. 25–30.*

Costume: A voluminous mother-hubbard which accentuates her size and does nothing else for her. She wears a broad-brimmed hat from which a number of keys dangle like tassels. It is held in place by a tremendous hat-pin. (See Prop List.)

MESSENGER: *A functionary. Long-legged, clear-voiced, and eager. About 20.*

Costume: Tights and jacket, again suggestive of Royal livery of some sort. He wears a dispatch case as a badge of office.

MUSICAL NUMBERS

ACT ONE, Scene I

Overture—toward the end, assisted by Tic, Tac, Toe
1. "Make Way for the King"—Ensemble
2. "Sing a Merry Song"—Nick
3. "It's a Dreadful Situation"—Tic, Tac, Toe
4. Repeat #3
5. "Pretend"—Nick, Penelope, Amelia, Celia, Arabella
6. "I'm a Great Magicianer"—Crunch
7. "Magic"—Crunch

ACT ONE, Scene II

8. "Pretend"—Penelope, Amelia, Celia, Arabella

ACT TWO

Overture—toward the end, assisted by Nick
9. "Here's a Tune We've Never Heard Of"—Tic, Tac, Toe
10. Repeat #9
11. "It's a Dreadful Situation"—Tic, Tac, Toe
12. "Make Way for the King"—Ensemble
13. "I'm a Great Magicianer"—Crunch
14. "Magic"—Crunch
15. "I'm a Wicked Rascal, Yes, I Am"—Crunch
16. "Magic"—Ensemble
17. "A Fool Would be Wise"—Penelope
18. Finale—Ensemble

Old King Cole

ACT ONE

SCENE I

THE SCENE: *The throne room of* KING COLE'S *castle. There are thrones at Right for the King and Queen, with a small table between them; a large toy chest up Left Center; miscellaneous chairs; and near the thrones, a rack for the scepter; a stool down Right; a bench Left Center. Conceptually, the stage is the castle; the auditorium is the kingdom itself. The two are joined by steps or, preferably, a kind of drawbridge.*

(OVERTURE.)

AT RISE: *The Overture is well into "Make Way for the King!"* AMELIA, CELIA *and* ARABELLA *are sitting on the floor around a large box of bright-colored papers. They are making party hats. Nearby,* MRS. SMEDLY *is sewing busily on a length of silken material. The* QUEEN *sits upon her throne, pasting sequins on a crown somewhat daintier than her own.*

TIC, TAC *and* TOE, *each with a mop, are scrubbing the floor and singing at the top of their lungs:*

TIC, TAC, TOE. *(Singing, to the tune of "Make Way for the King!")*

—Oh, we're shining up the floor,
'Cause we're getting ready for,
Yes, we're getting ready for a celebration!
And when the work is done,
We'll have a lot of—!

9

GROG. *(Off-stage, very loudly.)* Ho, there! Where is everybody?

(Everything stops abruptly except MRS. SMEDLY'S needle. GROG enters hurriedly up Left. He strongly resembles a traveling grab-bag. His many-pocketed clothes bulge with the clap-trap of his various offices; and on his back he wears a kind of quiver that contains his Jester's stick, Magician's wand, Doctor's thermometer (large-size), an 18-inch ruler and—in a special compartment—the King's bubble pipe. In his hand, he carries a large and ornate scepter. As he enters, he stumbles over the scepter and is kept from falling only by the quick action of the FIDDLERS.)

GROG. Ah! There you are! Well! Everybody up, now! Up!—
    (No one moves.)
Up, I say! Up, up, up, up!—Come now, hurry now!—Everybody *up!*

MRS. SMEDLY. Nonsense!

GROG. So?

MRS. SMEDLY. We can't be jumping up and down when there's work to do! Don't you know it's *Friday?*

GROG. Friday? *(He takes a calendar page from his pocket.)* Friday, you say?

MRS. SMEDLY. Not today! I mean the party. The party is on Friday!

GROG. Oh, I see— *(He throws the calendar page away and takes out a memo book.)* Yes, I've written it down: "On Friday, a party for the Princess!" No question about *that!* (He tears the page from the memo book and throws it away.) But the point is—

MRS. SMEDLY. —There won't *be* a party unless we get the work done!

GROG. No, no, no, no! That's not the point at all! The *point* is, it's eleven o'clock!

MRS. SMEDLY. Nonsense!

QUEEN. Eleven o'clock already?

GROG. *(Bows to her.)* Exactly, Your Majesty. It's exactly eleven o'clock. In fact— *(He consults a large pocket watch.)* —it's two minutes after. *(To MRS. SMEDLY.)* So you see, it can't be nonsense. It's time for the ceremony!

MRS. SMEDLY. But with so much to do—!

QUEEN. Yes, Grog, I think Mrs. Smedly is right. We needn't do it today. The King won't mind, I'm sure.

GROG. Of course, Your Majesty— But it's hardly a matter of minding or not minding. It's a matter of rules. And as Royal Regulator, I must remind you of the Regulation— *(He gives the scepter to* TIC *and takes a Book of Regulations from his pocket.)* So!—"Regulation 15. Court shall open each day at eleven o'clock with singing, laughter, pomp and circumstance." *(Putting the book away.)* There *is* a proper way to do these things—

QUEEN. I suppose so, but—

GROG. *(Reaching for the scepter.)* And as Prime Minister—!

   (TIC hands him a mop. He snatches the scepter impatiently and poses with it.)

As Prime Minister, I must tell you that what I say as Royal Regulator is perfectly correct. After all, a regulation *is* a regulation—and as far as that goes, a king is a king. He should have a proper introduction.

QUEEN. But everyone *knows* he's the king! And just this once—

GROG. No, Your Majesty. It's too-bad-and-I'm-very-sorry, but we'll have to do the ceremony. There's no question!

MRS. SMEDLY. All of it?

QUEEN. Why, yes! Can't we do just part of it? That would help some!

GROG. Part?—Well, it's possible, I suppose. The singing, of course, and the laughter—we'll *have* to do that. But because of the party and just this once, we *could* never-mind about the rest of it. We could do that, Your Majesty—

QUEEN. Then let's begin!—But *do* hurry, won't you?

(GROG *bows and turns to face the* OTHERS. *The* QUEEN
*pastes one more sequin onto the small crown and
then puts it down on the King's throne.*)

GROG. Up!
   (EVERYONE *rises.*)
That's it— *(He walks across the stage and poses; then
breaks out of it to peer at the* OTHERS.) Are we ready?
   (As EVERYONE *nods.*)
Steady, now!—Ready, now! *(He peers into the wings
and then resumes his official posture.)* So! *(He raps once
with the scepter.)* Make way for His Merry Majesty!—
King Cole, Ruler of the Kingdom of Haw!—Make way, I
say, for the King! *(Raps again, three times in rhythm.)*
                              (MUSIC CUE #1.)
   ALL. *(Song: "Make Way for the King!")*
            The King's coming in,
            The day will begin
            With pomp and with pageantry!
            Stand up when you sing,
            Make way for the King!
            Make way for His Majesty!—
      (Enter KING COLE *up Left. He bounces about, greet-
      ing each member of the court on his way to the
      throne—as the singing continues.)*
            There's a crown upon his head
            And it's very often said,
            He's a king by ev'ry royal definition!
            So give a royal cheer,
            His Highness is here,
            Make way for old King Cole!
      (They gather about the throne.)
            He's a proper sort of king,
            With a crown and everything,
            And a very merry royal disposition!
            So give a royal cheer,
            His Highness is here!
            Hooray for old King Cole!

(The song ends with a cheer. What follows is a continuation of the ceremony, rhythmic, with the responses in unison.)

KING COLE. Good morning, Court!
OTHERS. Good morning, Your Majesty!
KING COLE. Is everyone cheerful?
OTHERS. Oh, yes, Your Majesty!
KING COLE. Splendid!—Sing ha?
OTHERS. Ha-ha-ha-ha!
KING COLE. Sing hee?

(The QUEEN *tugs at his sleeve ineffectually.)*

OTHERS. Tee-hee-hee-hee!
KING COLE. Sing ho?
OTHERS. Ho-ho-ho-ho!
(The KING *joins in as they continue.)*
—ha-ha-ha-ha, tee-hee-hee-hee, ho-ha-ha-hee-hee-ho-ho-ho, etc.

(The laughter becomes less organized and more enthusiastic as it progresses. Everyone but the QUEEN *is in stitches. She finally captures the* KING'S *ear long enough to whisper into it.)*

KING COLE. *(Trying to hear her.)* What's that?— What say?— *(He finally holds up his hands for silence.)* Wait a minute!—Wait a minute!—Easy, now!—There!
(The court falls silent.)
Once more, my dear. What did you say?
QUEEN. That's enough!
KING COLE. Enough?—But we haven't done the pomp and circumstance!
QUEEN. There isn't time, dear. We've *so* much to do for the party, and— Well, Grog said the singing and laughter would be enough.
KING COLE. He did?
GROG. As Royal Regulator, Your Majesty, that was my advice.

KING COLE. And as Prime Minister?

GROG. I approved it.

KING COLE. Ah, well, then! I don't much care for the pomp and circumstance anyway! So it's all settled! *(He sits on the crown that the* QUEEN *has left on his throne and promptly jumps up.)* Ouch!

QUEEN. *(Rescuing the crown.)* Good heavens!—Do be careful, dear! You'll ruin Penelope's party crown!

KING COLE. Sorry, m'love— *(He discovers the* OTHERS *still standing about grinning at him and waves them away.)* Come, come, now!—On with the preparations!

(The OTHERS *scurry back to their work.* GROG *stops* AMELIA *and sends her to the toy chest for the* KING'S *bowl. He then puts the scepter in its rack and awaits the* KING'S *orders.* TIC, TAC *and* TOE *mop their way off up Left.)*

(In the meantime, the KING *has managed to stub his toe as he prepares to sit. He grabs the toe and calls after* MRS. SMEDLY.)* Oh, yes!—Mrs. Smedly!

MRS. SMEDLY. Your Majesty?

KING COLE. There's a lumpy sort of bump in the hall carpet, Mrs. Smedly. Will you see to it, please?

MRS. SMEDLY. At once, Your Majesty. *(She gathers up her sewing and exits up Left.)*

KING COLE. *(Settling himself on the throne.)* Now, then! My pipe, if you please—

*(*GROG *presents it to him with a flourish.)*

And my bowl?—Just so! Thank you, Amelia—

*(*AMELIA *puts the bowl on the table beside him, curtseys and goes back to her work.)*

(The KING *fills his pipe and motions to* GROG.*)* Is there any official business?

GROG. There is, Your Majesty. *(He takes out a sheet of paper.)*

(The KING *listens, blowing bubbles with his pipe.)* As Royal Regulator, I would like to report—

KING COLE. Oh, bother the Regulations! Isn't there something else?

GROG. Of course, Your Majesty— *(He throws the*

paper away and takes out another one.) As Royal Physician, then—

KING COLE. Is somebody sick? !

GROG. Oh, no, Your Majesty!

KING COLE. Well, then!—Give the report.

GROG. That *is* the report, sir. There's nobody sick. *(He throws the paper away.)*

KING COLE. Splendid!—Anything else?

GROG. *(Taking out a large, folded paper.)* The party, Your Majesty. As Court Jester and Royal Party Planner, I have made a plan— *(He unfolds it to display a mad, multi-colored diagram, complete with obscure algebraic formulae.)*

KING COLE. *(Impressed.)* My goodness!

QUEEN. *(Stops working to look.)* What a lovely plan!

GROG. Thank you, Your Majesty— As you can see, there'll be ice cream, cake, lollipops, salted peanuts, sugar-plums and sassparilla— And over here— Guests!

KING COLE. Excellent!

GROG. The trouble is, I can't be sure of the number. I don't know about Crunch, you see—

QUEEN. About who?

GROG. Crunch, Your Majesty, the Royal Fiddle Polisher. He won't say he's coming, but then again, he won't say he's not coming. When I mentioned the party, he growled.

KING COLE. *(Putting down his pipe.)* Growled? !

GROG. *(Demonstrating.)* Grrrrr!

QUEEN. Oh!

KING COLE. Good heavens!—Where *is* Crunch?

GROG. Well, sir, he's not here—not that I can see. So he must be somewhere else. But if he's not *there*, why, then he's neither here nor there, and I wash my hands of him!—I don't much like being growled at.

QUEEN. Goodness! I should think not!

KING COLE. Of course he may have been upset about something—bit of a headache, wrong side of bed, something like that. Or he may have had trouble polishing the fiddles. They *do* get dusty, and—

GROG. Fiddles!

KING COLE. Uh—fiddles?

GROG. (*Peering at the plan.*) Of course, Your Majesty! The fiddlers should be rehearsing!—It's here someplace— So!—Music for the party!

QUEEN. Oh, yes! We have to have music!

KING. *And* a rehearsal! Several rehearsals, by jingo!— Call the fiddlers!

GROG. (*Bows, then turns to shout off.*) Fiddlers ho!— The King calls for his—!?

(*He stops abruptly, cocking his head as* NICK *enters from the back of the house and comes down the aisle whistling "Sing a Merry Song." He is all hero, but young. He carries his belongings wrapped in a bright bandana.*)

QUEEN. (*Uncertainly.*) Fiddlers?

KING COLE. (*Getting up.*) No, my dear, it's something else!

GROG. (*Pointing.*) Out there, Your Majesty! In the kingdom!

(*They come down to the front of the stage.* AMELIA, CELIA *and* ARABELLA *scurry after them, giggling and whispering excitedly as* NICK *reaches the foot of the drawbridge and stops.*)

NICK. Hello, the castle!

GROG. Hello yourself!

KING COLE. Goodness, I've never seen *him* before! See what he wants.

GROG. What do you want, young man?

NICK. Not much, sir. My name is Nick, and I'm seeking my fortune. May I come in?

GROG. He wants to come in.

KING COLE. There's no harm in that, by jingo! Let him in!

QUEEN. But not just yet! We mustn't be standing about

like this— And he *should* be announced! *(To* GROG.) Shouldn't he?

GROG. By all means, Your Majesty. It's in the Regulations!

QUEEN. *(Taking the* KING's *hand.)* Come, dear.

(They hurry back to their thrones. GROG *shooes away the* LADIES-IN-WAITING, *who line up near their workbox, giggling excitedly. The* KING *waves a go-ahead signal.)*

GROG. All right, young man—
(As NICK *arrives on stage.)*
Your name is Nick?

NICK. *(Glancing about nervously.)* Well—Nicholas, really.

GROG. Yes— That sounds better, I think, for being announced and all. More dignified. *(He turns to address the* KING *and* QUEEN *but stops as he sees the scepter in its rack.)* Oh, bother! *(He crosses quickly to get the scepter, then returns half-way to* NICK.) Now, then— *(He raps with the scepter.)* If it please the court, one Nicholas of—? *(To* NICK.) Where are you from?

NICK. Well, I—I was close to a river yesterday. The day before that, I was picking wild flowers in a big meadow. I'm not sure just where it was, I'm afraid—

GROG. No matter— *(Resuming his official stance.)* One Nicholas of Nowhere desires an audience with His Merry Majesty, King Cole of the Kingdom of Haw!

KING COLE. Splendid!—Come here, my boy.

GROG. *(As* NICK *goes by him.)* And don't forget to bow!

NICK. *(Bows awkwardly.)* Good morning, Your Majesties.

KING COLE. Uh—good morning, Nick— Won't you sit down?

GROG. Not yet, Your Majesty!

QUEEN. Ask him what he wants, dear. That comes first.

KING COLE. So it does!—Sorry, m'love— *(To* NICK.) Now, then, Nick, what can we do for you?

NICK. Well, sir— If it's not too much to ask, sir, I'm looking for a job.

KING COLE. A job? !

NICK. Yes, sir.

KING COLE. Are you sure you don't mean money? Or the hand of the Princess? That's what people usually ask for.

NICK. Oh, no, Your Majesty! If I have a job, I can earn all the money I need, and— Well, sir, I didn't even know there *was* a Princess.

KING COLE. Fancy that!

GROG. There's always a Princess, young man. Or a Prince. In this kingdom, it's a Princess. Everybody knows that!

QUEEN. But he *is* a stranger, Grog. It's quite possible he's never heard of her. *(To* NICK.*)* Her name's Penelope.

KING COLE. And she's a fine girl, by jingo! The fact is, we're getting ready to give her a coming-out party!

NICK. Coming-out, sir?

QUEEN. It means she's coming out of short dresses and pigtails and things like that. You see, she's not a child any more, she's a young lady.

KING COLE. And it's going to be a dandy party, Nick. Would you like to come?

NICK. Thank you, Your Majesty, but—well, I'd *rather* have a job, sir, if it's all right.

KING COLE. Certainly! Everyone should have a job! *(To* GROG.*)* Do we have any jobs?

GROG. Well, he might take one of mine, Your Majesty —one of the smaller ones. I don't like to complain, but I have felt a bit rushed lately—a little breathless, you know, getting from one thing to another— So if he were to be the Court Fool— Uh—the Royal Jester, I mean— Something like that—

KING COLE. Excellent! The very thing!

GROG. *(To* NICK.*)* Do you know anything about jesting?

NICK. Not very much, I guess. But I'm a good worker, and—

KING COLE. Oh, come, now! You must know something! Not even a joke?

NICK. Well—yes, I do know a joke. Not a very good one. It's a kind of riddle.

GROG. So?

NICK. Why does a baby chick walk softly?

KING COLE. Well, now, let me see— Why *does* a baby chick walk softly?

NICK. If it please Your Majesty—because he can't walk, hardly.

KING COLE. By jingo! *(He laughs merrily.)*

GROG. Your Majesty— *(He waits for the KING to control himself.)* Your Majesty, it's *not* very funny.

KING COLE. No, I don't suppose so. But it does show promise!

GROG. Is that *all* you know?

NICK. Well, I—I know how to skip and things like that—and the beginning of a song or two.

GROG. Just the beginning?

KING COLE. You ought to know more than just the beginning, I should think.

NICK. It doesn't much matter, sir. Once you get a tune started, the rest comes along by itself.

KING COLE. Really?

NICK. It does with me, anyway. As long as you keep it merry, sir, there's nothing to it!   *(MUSIC CUE #2.)*

Song: *"Sing a Merry Song"*

Begin to sing a merry song,
And bluebells ring-a-ling along;
Ev'ry young pollywog
Tries to jump like a frog
When you start to sing a merry song!

(He moves about, hand-arounding with the LADIES-IN-WAITING *and ending back at the throne. The* OTHERS *may join in, singing or humming, as the song goes on.)*

It's fun to hum a merry tune!
The clouds play tag around the moon;
Ev'ry star in the sky

Winks a bright, golden eye
When you start to hum a merry tune!
The sunbeams dance a merry jig!
The world is not so very big:
It will fit in your hand,
It's a magical land
When you're singing—so sing a merry song!

KING COLE. Well, now!—What do you think, Grog?

GROG. Jolly, Your Majesty. No question about *that.*—I don't think he's funny enough to be Royal Jester, but he could learn, possibly. And I *could* use an assistant. I could do that, I suppose—

KING COLE. Splendid! *(Takes the scepter and touches it to the top of* NICK'S *head.)* You are hereby appointed Royal Apprentice to the Royal Jester and Royal Assistant to Grog!—That covers it, I think. *(He puts the scepter into its rack.)* Welcome to the court!

NICK. Golly, Your Majesty!

KING COLE. You've met the Queen, of course—
*(*NICK *bows as the* QUEEN *nods and smiles.)*
And Grog, the Prime Minister *and* the Royal Regulator—

NICK. Yes, sir.

KING COLE. *(Leading him to them.)* And these are the ladies-in-waiting. Amelia—
(She curtseys. GROG *hops into place beyond her, waving his magic wand.)*
And— Oh, yes! Grog, the Royal Magician—
*(*GROG *steps quickly beyond* CELIA *after his bow, taking out his thermometer.)*
Celia—
(She curtseys.)
And Grog, the Royal Physician.
*(*GROG *bows and moves on as before, trading the thermometer for his Jester's stick.)*
And this is Arabella—
(As they move on, GROG *cuts a caper in front of them. The* KING *chuckles, delighted.)*
And Grog, Nick— Grog, the Court Fool!
(As GROG *freezes, reacting to the word.)*

Or Jester, I should say! Grog, the Royal Jester.

 (GROG smiles and makes a comic bow which NICK returns in kind.)

Splendid, Nick! Very good! Why, we'll make a Fool of you in no time!

 NICK. Thank you, Your Majesty.

 KING COLE. Now, that's everyone, I think, except for Mrs. Smedly, the Royal Castlekeeper—the fiddlers, of course, and—

 GROG. *(Remembering)* Fiddlers! Where *are* those fiddlers! *(He starts off to look for them but is stopped by a great commotion off-stage. TIC, TAC, TOE and CRUNCH enter abruptly up Left, pushing, shoving, yipping and growling.)* So *there* you are!

(The tumbling group comes to a halt, the FIDDLERS forming a half-circle around CRUNCH, who glares at everyone angrily.)

 KING COLE. Good heavens!—

 QUEEN. What *have* you been doing?

(The FIDDLERS immediately begin to sing heatedly, each using different words:)

 TIC. *(Singing.)*

  If it please Your Royal Highness—

 TAC. *(Singing, at the same time.)*

  We were searching for the fiddles—

 TOE. *(Also singing at the same time.)*

  We don't like to point the finger—

 GROG. One at a time!—Now, then! *(To the KING.)* You'd better sit down, Your Majesty. It may be official.

 KING COLE. Of course! *(He scurries back to the throne and sits.)*

 GROG. *(Announcing.)* The Royal Fiddlers, Your Majesty!—And Crunch, the Royal Fiddle Polisher!

(The FIDDLERS bow and force CRUNCH to do so by pushing down his head.)

King Cole. Well, now!—That is— What seems to be the trouble?

Tic, Tac, Toe. Your Majesty!   *(MUSIC CUE #3.)*
　　　Song: "It's a Dreadful Situation"
　　　It's a dreadful situation,
　　　It's a frightful complication,
　　　It's a very sorry sort of mess!
　　　We were feeling hale and hearty,
　　　Getting ready for the party,
　　　When we found this wicked wickedness!

Tic. *(Sings.)*
　　　Someone faddled all the fiddles!

Tac. *(Sings.)*
　　　Fiddle-faddled all the fiddles!

Toe. *(Sings.)*
　　　Fiddle-faddled ev'ry fiddle there!

Tic, Tac, Toe. *(Sing together.)*
　　　We're no good at solving riddles,
　　　But he says he made the fiddles,
　　　Made the fiddles vanish into air!

King Cole. You mean the fiddles are gone?

Queen. *(As the Fiddlers nod excitedly.)* But they can't be gone! We need them for the party!

Grog. And he couldn't have done it by magic, if that's what you mean! After all, *I'm* the Court Magician!

King Cole. My goodness! Are you *sure* the fiddles have disappeared?

Tic, Tac, Toe. *(Singing energetically.)*
　　　　　　　　　　　(MUSIC CUE #4.)
　　　Someone faddled all the fiddles,
　　　Fiddle-faddled all the fiddles,
　　　Made the royal fiddles disappear!
　　　We're no good at solving riddles,
　　　But the faddler of the fiddles,
　　　He's the one that's standing over here!

King Cole. Crunch?

Tic. *(Sings.)*
　　　It's a dreadful situation!

TAC. *(Sings.)*
>We can't prove the accusation!

TOE. *(Sings.)*
>But we think the evidence is clear!

TIC, TAC, TOE. *(Sing together.)*
>If you ask him, he'll admit it,
>He says he's the one who did it,
>He's the one who made them disappear!

KING COLE. By jingo!

CRUNCH. *(Bows mockingly as they ALL stare at him.)* If it please the court, I am a great magician.

KING COLE. Now, don't talk nonsense, Crunch! It doesn't please the court at all if you've faddled the fiddles! My goodness! Why would you do such a thing?

CRUNCH. Because, Your Majesty, I don't like to polish fiddles!

QUEEN. But that's your job!

KING COLE. And you've never complained about it—not that I know of—

CRUNCH. But I have grumbled, Your Majesty—in corners, and such as that. And I've decided it's time for a change.

GROG. *You've* decided!

CRUNCH. I should like to be appointed Royal Magician—

KING COLE. Good heavens!

CRUNCH. And if I can make fiddles disappear— Well, it's no trick to start in on other things. So you'll be wise to do as I ask.

GROG. Oh, now, really!—This will never do, Your Majesty! For one thing, we already have a Royal Magician—and a very good one, too, if you ask me! For another thing, we can't have people going around admitting things just because they want to! This is not only serious, Your Majesty, it's also official! If Crunch is accused of something—which he certainly should be—why, then, he has to have a trial! It's in the Regulations!

KING COLE. Well—if it's in the Regulations, of course—

MRS. SMEDLY. *(Bustles in up Left carrying something in her apron.)* Your Majesty! Your Majesty!—

GROG. In due time, Mrs. Smedly! Please!

MRS. SMEDLY. But—!

GROG. Please, Mrs. Smedly! In *due* time!—Where's my assistant?

NICK. Here, sir!

GROG. Bring me the scepter!

(NICK *does so as the* OTHERS *arrange themselves for the trial.*)

That's it— Now, hold this. *(He takes the scepter and gives* NICK *the Book of Regulations which is open. He raps with the scepter.)* The trial will now begin! *(To* CRUNCH.) Give your name and occupation.

CRUNCH. Grrr!

GROG. *(Jumping back a bit.)* His name, Your Majesty, is Crunch.

KING COLE. Oh, we know all that. Go on to something else!

GROG. If it please the court, the prisoner is accused of the following crimes, misdemeanors and bad things: One! The crime of fiddle-faddle, for having faddled the fiddles. *(Referring to the Book of Regulations.)* Two! Practicing magic without a license!—which is a misdemeanor. And three—if I may, Your Majesty—growling at the Prime Minister, a bad thing! *(He raps with the scepter.)* The Royal Fiddlers will now testify.

(The FIDDLERS *line up and bow to the throne.)*

TIC. First, Your Majesty, the fiddles are gone.

TAC. Second, we can't find them.

TOE. Third, they must have been faddled!

GROG. *(Raps with the scepter.)* Guilty!

KING COLE. He is?

GROG. He admits it, Your Majesty.

KING COLE. Oh, yes! I'd forgotten.

GROG. So now we can go on to practicing magic without a license.

QUEEN. But he admits that too, doesn't he?

GROG. So he does, Your Majesty! *(Rapping the scepter.)* Guilty again!

MRS. SMEDLY. Oh, but he's not!

GROG. *Not* guilty?

MRS. SMEDLY. *(Coming forward.)* Of course not! Magic, indeed! Does this look like magic?

(She opens her apron to display bits and pieces of three fiddles. GROG reaches into the debris and holds up a fiddle-string from which a fiddle-head dangles. There is general consternation.)

TIC, TAC, TOE. *(Peering into the apron.)* Fiddle-sticks!

QUEEN. Good heavens!

KING COLE. He's chopped them to bits!

MRS. SMEDLY. And put them under the hall carpet, Your Majesty. There was a lumpy sort of bump there, just as you said—

KING COLE. Indeed there was, Mrs. Smedly. *Exactly* as I said!

MRS. SMEDLY. And the lump in the bump— Well, you can see what it was, Your Majesty. He didn't use magic at all! In fact, *I* think he used an axe!

KING COLE. By jingo! *(To* CRUNCH.) Is this true?

CRUNCH. Well, I *could* have done it by magic. It just takes longer.

GROG. But the point is, you didn't!—That's the point, Your Majesty! He's not only guilty of fiddle-faddle, he's also guilty of faddle-fibbing!

KING COLE. Of what?

GROG. Fabble-fibbling, Your Majesty! Fibble-fabbling! Fibbing about the faddling! What I mean is— *(He raps sharply with the scepter.)* He told a lie!

ALL. *(Horrified.)* A lie! *(They draw back, staring at* CRUNCH, *as they realize the magnitude of his crime.)*

GROG. And he'll have to be punished! *(He consults the Book of Regulations.)*

KING COLE. Oh, dear, yes!—It was bad enough that

you faddled the fiddles, Crunch, but a lie—! That's a *very* bad thing. A *terrible* thing! We can't have people telling lies!

CRUNCH. Very well, Your Majesty. Do what you like. But I *am* a great magician! You'll see! And you'll be sorry!

KING COLE. Oh, I am sorry! Goodness! I *don't* much like to punish people. But— Well, there's no help for it now, I'm afraid. *(To* GROG.*)* Read the punishment.

GROG. It's a very short sentence, Your Majesty—one word. *(Reads from the Book.)* Banishment!

(There is a general murmur of awe.)
*(*GROG *raps with the scepter.)* The King will pronounce the sentence!

KING COLE. *(Stands and enunciates clearly.)* Ban-ish-ment!—According to law and because of telling a lie, you are hereby and forthwith banished from the Kingdom of Haw! That means goodbye-to-you, Crunch, and don't-forget-your-suitcase.

GROG. *(Raps with the scepter.)* Take him away!

(The FIDDLERS *do so up Left.)*

QUEEN. *(Jumping up.)* But what about the fiddles? We have to have fiddles! If we don't have music for the par-ty—! *(Wails.)* The *party!*

KING COLE. There, there, m'love!

QUEEN. Oh, it just ruins everything! *(She exits abrupt-ly up Left, sobbing.)*

MRS. SMEDLY. Your Majesty! *(She pauses to dump the fiddle-sticks into the box of colored papers and runs off after the* QUEEN.*)*

KING COLE. Oh, my goodness! *(Trotting after them.)* Please, my dear!—Wait a minute!—I'm sure we'll think of something! *(He exits.)*

GROG. *(Indignantly.)* But Your Majesty!—You can't just—!
    (He sees the LADIES-IN-WAITING, *who have picked up the box of papers and are on their way out with it.)*

Oh, now, look here!
        (*The* LADIES-IN-WAITING *exit up Left.*)
(GROG *looks about wildly and stares at* NICK, *frustrated.*)
Fiddles! (*He snatches the Book of Regulations and starts
off. Near the exit, he stops, remembering his official duty.
He turns and raps with the scepter.*) The Court is
adjourned! (*He exits.*)

NICK. (*Staring after him.*) Golly! (*He looks about—
and continues to look, becoming more and more inter-
ested in his surroundings. His eyes stop at the throne. He
hesitates, then goes to it and examines it carefully. He
climbs up to sit in the* KING'S *place, gingerly at first, but
with increasing confidence and enjoyment. He finds the
party crown that the* QUEEN *has left behind. He puts it
on. Next, he discovers the* KING'S *bubble pipe. He tries
it out. He sits comfortably, blowing bubbles and pausing
now and then to dismiss an imaginary dignitary with a
regal gesture. His game is interrupted by the sound of
approaching* VOICES, *all of them talking at once in un-
intelligible excitement. He scrambles down from the
throne and stands self-consciously beside it, the crown
still on his head.*)

(*The following exchange is off-stage, very rapid, and only
vaguely understandable.*)

AMELIA. —All because he wanted to be Court Magician!
CELIA. Imagine!
ARABELLA. And you missed the whole thing!
AMELIA. And then it turned out he hadn't used magic
at all!
CELIA. Not at all!
ARABELLA. And he lied about it!

(*At the last moment,* NICK *remembers the crown. He
        puts it back where he found it and resumes his posi-
        tion just as* AMELIA, CELIA, *and* ARABELLA *enter up
        Left with* PENELOPE. *A Princess is a Princess, of
        course, but at the moment—so far as her general*

appearance is concerned—PENELOPE *might very well be one more lady-in-waiting.)*

AMELIA. Isn't it dreadful?
CELIA. Oh, it is!
ARABELLA. And just before the party!
AMELIA. The Queen says there might not even be a party!
CELIA. No party at all!
ARABELLA. Without any fiddles—
PENELOPE. *(Sees* NICK.) Oh!

(The OTHERS *stare at her uncertainly.)*

AMELIA. What's the matter?

(PENELOPE *points at* NICK. *The* OTHERS *turn to look at him.)*

NICK. *(Self-consciously.)* Hello.
CELIA. Oh, it's you!
ARABELLA. What are *you* doing here?
NICK. Nothing. Just waiting, I guess.
AMELIA. Oh, but you can't do that!
CELIA. Not at all!
ARABELLA. *We're* the ladies-in-waiting. That's *our* job.
PENELOPE. But who is he?
AMELIA. You see? You missed all of it!
CELIA. Oh, you *did!*
ARABELLA. His name is Nick. And he's the new apprentice Jester.
PENELOPE. An apprentice?
NICK. Just temporarily. I'm in training to be a Fool. What's *your* name?
PENELOPE. Penny.
NICK. I'm very glad to meet you.
PENELOPE. Are you coming to the party?
NICK. Are you?
PENELOPE. Oh, yes! I almost have to.

(The LADIES-IN-WAITING *find all this vastly amusing and giggle madly among themselves.)*

NICK. *(Self-consciously.)* Then— Well, I—I guess I'd like to, all right. If there *is* one.

PENELOPE. Oh, I'm sure there will be. Only—well, it *won't* be the same, of course, if we don't have the fiddles.

AMELIA. That's the worst thing. It won't be the same at all!

CELIA. Oh, it *won't!*

ARABELLA. We just *have* to have fiddles!

NICK. *(Shrugs.)* That's easy enough.

PENELOPE. It is?

NICK. Sure. Make them up!

AMELIA. *(Impressed.)* You mean by magic?

CELIA. *Magic?*

NICK. Well—it's a kind of magic, I guess—

ARABELLA. Can *you* do it?

NICK. Oh, anybody can do it. It's just— Well, it's just pretending. You can do anything that way.

PENELOPE. Can you *really?*

NICK. Sure you can!   *(MUSIC CUE #5.)*
                    Song: *"Pretend"*
          Pretend, and it's all up to you.
          There's no end to the things you can do!
          There's nothing to it,
          I can do it,
          You can do it, too!
          Pretending is all you have to do—
(To the LADIES-IN-WAITING.)
          Pretend you can fiddle-diddle-dee—
LADIES-IN-WAITING. *(Singing; pretending to fiddle.)*
          Fiddle-lie, fiddle-lum, fiddle-lee!
NICK.
          There's nothing to it,
          You can do it,
          Just you wait and see!
LADIES-IN-WAITING.
          A fee, fiddle-diddle-diddle-dee!

(They continue the pantomime, humming, as the music becomes a waltz. NICK and PENELOPE dance one chorus, at the end of which she mounts the throne. On the repetition, she sings:)

PENELOPE. *(Putting on the crown as the OTHERS bow. Sings.)*
> Pretend I'm a queen—and behold!
> I've a palace of silver and gold!

(To NICK.) But could we still pretend?
> Would you be my friend?
> If it really were true?
> If I were a queen, could I still waltz with you?

NICK. *(Jumps up on the throne beside her.)* Sure! *(Singing.)*
> Why, I'll be a king on a throne!
> With a palace or two of my own!
> There's nothing to it,
> I can do it,
> Just you wait and see!
> A king on a throne is what I'll be!

ALL. *(Singing.)*
> Pretend and it's all up to you!
> There's no end to the things you can do!
> There's nothing to it,
> You can do it,
> Just you wait and see!
> Pretending—you're anything you want to be!

(As the song ends, enter MRS. SMEDLY.)

MRS. SMEDLY. Penelope Cole!
PENELOPE. Oh, dear!

(The LADIES-IN-WAITING take one look at MRS. SMEDLY and exit hastily up Left. NICK jumps down from the throne and starts to follow them, but stops self-consciously, watching PENELOPE.)

MRS. SMEDLY. *(Advancing.)* —You get down from there this very minute! You know you shouldn't play on the throne!—The idea!

PENELOPE. We were just—just pretending, Mrs. Smedly—

MRS. SMEDLY. Well, that's all very fine, I'm sure, but— *(Suddenly aware that* PENELOPE *is wearing her party crown.)* Princess!—Oh, you shouldn't be wearing it now! That's your *party* crown!

PENELOPE. *(Surrendering the crown; meekly.)* I'm sorry, Mrs. Smedly—

MRS. SMEDLY. I've never seen such a day! Everything at sixes and sevens, sevens and eights— Goodness! *(Motions to* PENELOPE *and starts out.)* Come along, now! Your mother wants you— And we've millions of things to do— Millions and billions!—Oh, we've so much to *do!* *(She exits up Left.)*

NICK. *(As* PENELOPE *hesitates.)* She said— You mean— You really are a—a Princess?

PENELOPE. *(Nods self-consciously.)* It's—it's all right, isn't it?

MRS. SMEDLY. *(Calling from off-stage.)* Princess?

*(*PENELOPE *looks once more at* NICK *and then runs off after* MRS. SMEDLY.)*

NICK. Golly!
　　*(*GROG *enters behind him, his nose buried in a large book. He is almost running. He bangs into* NICK *unexpectedly.)*
Oh!

GROG. So! *(Frowning at* NICK *over the top of the book.)* It's you, is it? Well, come along, young man! I need a little assisting! *(He resumes his swift journey across the room,* NICK *following.)*

NICK. Yes, sir!—What are we going to do, sir?

GROG. *(Stopping abruptly.)* Do? Why, fiddles, of course! Fiddles! *(They exit down Right.)*
　　　　　　　　　　　　　(MUSIC CUE #6.)

(Immediately, CRUNCH sticks his head into the room. He looks about and then enters stealthily down Left. He carries a bulging carpetbag, from which bits of clothing protrude. An umbrella is strapped to the outside. He puts down the bag, makes sure he is alone, and exits. In a moment, he re-enters, carrying a large and rather ornate box. He takes it to the toy chest and puts it down. From his pocket he takes a stringed tag and ties it to the handle at one end of the box. Apparently satisfied, he stands back to admire his handiwork, chuckling to himself.)

CRUNCH. Magic!—It's magic they want, eh?—Who says I don't know any magic!
        Song: "I'm a Great Magicianer"
        I know the secret history
        Of ev'ry kind of mystery;
        I know the what and whichery
        Of magic and of witchery!
                So just look out
                When I'm about!
        I'm a great magician, yes, I am!
(He whips out a handkerchief, wads it in his fist and makes a pass over it. He opens his fist triumphantly—and the handkerchief is still there. Quickly, he puts it away and goes on with the song.)
        Oh, I'm a great magicianer,
        A super superstitioner,
        A magic exhibitioner,
        A hobble-gobble-itioner!
                They banished me,
                But they will see!
        I'm a great magician, yes, I am!
(He goes to the box, mumbling, chuckling, rubbing his hands in excitement.) Oh, they'll be sorry!—Banish *me*, will they?—Just wait till they see *this!* *(He tries the lid of the box. It will not open. He chuckles even more.)* Oh, here's a wondrous sort of box! Here's a box that *is* a box! Here's a box that really *locks!*—Oh, it's magic, is it?

We'll see who's a magician!—Well! *(He stops and hums a bit experimentally.)*
      Ah! That's it!—Now!
(He strikes a pose and recites:)   *(MUSIC CUE #7.)*
      Here's a wondrous magic box!
      Oh, here's a box to think about!
      For when it shuts, it always locks;
      And what goes in will not come out!
      Oh, here's a wondrous magic thing!
      Here's a charm that cannot miss!
      To break the spell, you have to sing
      A magic song that goes like this:
(Energetically, hopping about.)
      Magic! Magic!
      Lolly-dolly-dolly-did!
      Magic! Magic!
      Open up the lid!
(The lid springs open—or, if necessary, CRUNCH opens it. He is delighted. He shuts the lid and tries it again:)
      Magic! Magic!
      Lolly-dolly-dolly-did!
      Magic! Magic!
      Open up the lid!
(The lid springs open again. He pats the box happily, leaving it open.) Oh, ho! There we are!—Now we're ready for them! *(He picks up his carpet-bag and shakes a fist at the throne.)* Banished, am I?—You'll be sorry for *that!* *(He scurries to the drawbridge and exits into the house and up the aisle, mumbling, grumbling, chuckling and growling. As he does so, the LIGHTS on stage dim, marking the*

END OF THE SCENE

ACT ONE

SCENE II

THE SCENE: *The same, later in the day. There is no*

curtain. As CRUNCH *makes his exit at the back of the house, the LIGHTS come up again on stage. The* LADIES-IN-WAITING *enter up Left, their arms loaded with finished party hats which they mean to put away in the toy chest. They are giggling and talking among themselves.*

AMELIA. *(As they enter.)* He didn't even know she *was* the Princess!

CELIA. Oh, he *didn't!*

ARABELLA. And when Mrs. Smedly said—! *(She stops abruptly as she sees the box.)*

    (AMELIA *and* CELIA *follow her gaze, and they stand there for a moment, staring.)*
What's that do you think?

AMELIA. Well, it—it looks like some sort of box!

CELIA. Oh, a beautiful box!

ARABELLA. But where did it come from? *(She advances cautiously.)*

AMELIA. *(Following her.)* Is there anything in it?

CELIA. *Is* there?

ARABELLA. *(Looking into the box.)* Not a thing!—Do you think we should *do* something?

AMELIA. *I* think so! *(To* CELIA.) We'd better call Mrs. Smedly!

CELIA. Oh, we should! *(She starts to go, but stops as she discovers the hats she is carrying. She adds them to* AMELIA'S *load and runs off up Left.)*

ARABELLA. *(In the meantime,* ARABELLA *examines the box, working her way to the end of it. Finding the tag.)* Look!—There's a tag!

AMELIA. Can you read it?

ARABELLA. Well— No, but— *(She looks briefly for a place to put the hats she carries and finally gives them to* AMELIA.) Here! *(She turns the tag so she can read it.)* Oh, dear! It's—it's from Crunch!

AMELIA. Crunch! ?

ARABELLA. And it's *for* the King!—Do you think we should call him?—Should we?

AMELIA. Oh, yes! Oh, dear, yes! *(Again the business with the hats.)* Here! *(She gives them all to* ARABELLA *and runs off.)*

*(*ARABELLA *balances the load precariously. She manages to open the door of the toy chest and to put the hats inside, all the time trying to keep her distance from the box. As she closes the door,* CELIA *re-enters with* MRS. SMEDLY, *followed by* TIC, TAC *and* TOE.)*

MRS. SMEDLY. Box, indeed! Haven't we enough to do without—? *(As she sees it.)* Good heavens! It *is* a box!

ARABELLA. *(Pointing to the tag excitedly.)* From Crunch, Mrs. Smedly, it's from Crunch! It says so!

MRS. SMEDLY. Nonsense! *(She hurries over to read the tag.)*

(The OTHERS *crowd around, buzzing with excitement.)*

Well, I declare!

(Enter KING COLE *and* AMELIA, *followed by the* QUEEN *and* PENELOPE.)*

KING COLE. A box, you say? A box? What kind of box?

MRS. SMEDLY. *(Turning to meet him.)* Your Majesty, it seems to be a Crunch box!

(The OTHERS *stand back so he can see it.)*

KING COLE. By jingo! *(He examines it carefully, the* QUEEN *close behind him.)*

*(*PENELOPE *joins the* LADIES-IN-WAITING. MRS. SMEDLY *stands with the tag in her hand.)*

(The KING *completes his inspection and looks at her.)*

Are you sure it's from Crunch?

MRS. SMEDLY. That's what it says, Your Majesty.

QUEEN. Goodness! What else does it say?

KING COLE. Yes, yes, Mrs. Smedly, does it say anything else?

MRS. SMEDLY. Well— Perhaps I'd better read it to

you. *(She does so.)* "Dear Your Majesty: I am sorry for what I did. I don't much like being banished, but to show you there are no hard feelings, I would like to give you this box. It is a very good box for putting things in. Yours very truly, Crunch."

KING COLE. Do you hear that, my dear? It's a present! Isn't that nice?

QUEEN. Well, yes, it *is* very nice—

KING COLE. Perhaps I shouldn't have banished him after all.

MRS. SMEDLY. Oh, but he *did* tell a lie, Your Majesty.

QUEEN. And he *did* faddle the fiddles!

TIC, TAC, TOE. That's true, Your Majesty! *(Singing energetically.)*

> Someone faddled all the fiddles,
> Fiddle-faddled all the fiddles,
> Made the royal fiddles disappear!

KING COLE. *(Stopping them.)* Yes, yes, yes! We've *done* all that!

QUEEN. But we still don't have any fiddles—and that's the important thing— *(Sniffling a little.)* All we have is a—a box!

KING COLE. Of course, my dear, but— Well— *(Brightening.)* Maybe it's a music box!

MRS. SMEDLY. I don't think so, Your Majesty—

KING COLE. *(To the* FIDDLERS, *hopefully.)* But it might be! ?

TIC, TAC, TOE. No, Your Majesty.

KING COLE. Well— Perhaps not, then— But it *is* a box, my dear. That's better than nothing!

GROG. *(Entering down Right.)* Your Majesty!
(They ALL *turn to look at him.)*
(He bows.) Your Majesty, I have done it! As Royal Magician— *(He lets the sentence die, frowning.)* Ho! What's all this?—A box?

KING COLE. You see? Just as I was saying! *(As* GROG *investigates the box.)* It's a present from Crunch.

GROG. So?

QUEEN. To—to show he's sorry for what he did.

KING COLE. Isn't that splendid?

GROG. Well—it's only a box, of course. It's not the same as fiddles.

QUEEN. *(Bursting into tears.)* Fiddles!—Ohhhh!—Ohhhh!

KING COLE. Oh, my goodness!—There, my dear! There, there, there!

GROG. Please, Your Majesty! What I mean to say is, I *have* the fiddles!

(There is a general reaction. The QUEEN *stops sobbing abruptly.)*

KING COLE. You—you have them? *(As* GROG *bows proudly.)* By jingo!

GROG. As Royal Magician, Your Majesty, I soaked the pieces of the old fiddles in a secret magic brine. The result was—

QUEEN. *(Happily.)* New fiddles!

GROG. Not exactly, Your Majesty.—Pickled pieces. As Royal Magician, I failed— But as Prime Minister—! Oh-ho! That's something else again! As Prime Minister, I went to the fiddle-maker's shop! *(He claps his hands and* NICK *enters down Right carrying three Haw-type, one-string fiddles.)* Fiddles, Your Majesty! Bought and paid for!

(MUSIC CUE #8.)

ALL. *(General rejoicing, ad lib.)* Hooray!—Long live Grog!—Hooray for the fiddles!

(There is a rush towards NICK *and the fiddles that leaves* GROG *more or less isolated.* EVERYONE *crowds about, the* FIDDLERS *first of all. The* LADIES-IN-WAITING *and* PENELOPE *skip in and out among the* OTHERS, *singing at full tilt.)*

PENELOPE *and the* LADIES-IN-WAITING.
    Pretend you can fiddle-diddle-dee!
    Fiddle-lie, fiddle-lum, fiddle-lee!
    There's nothing to it,
    We can do it!

GROG. Wait a minute!—Easy, now!—Hold on, I say! *(He pushes his way through the* OTHERS *and stands in front of* NICK *as though to protect him and the fiddles.)* Whoa!

KING COLE. Is there something wrong?

GROG. Not wrong, Your Majesty. No, I wouldn't say that. What I *would* say is be careful! If it please the court, there are no more fiddles. What's more, the fiddle-maker is going on vacation, so there won't *be* any more for a long time.

QUEEN. But we don't need any more!

KING COLE. I shouldn't think so. We've only three Fiddlers.

GROG. But we do need these, Your Majesty. The point is, if anything should happen to *these* fiddles—

QUEEN. Oh!—Oh, dear!

GROG. Exactly! So we can't be bouncing and jouncing and all that sort of thing. We have to be careful! And we *should* have a safe place to keep them.

KING COLE. That's true, of course—

MRS. SMEDLY. The box?

GROG. No, no, Mrs. Smedly! The fiddles!

MRS. SMEDLY. I *mean* the fiddles! Couldn't we put them in the box? After all, it is a box for putting things in.

KING COLE. By jingo, so it is!—Couldn't we put them in the box?

GROG. Well—I suppose so. Yes, we can do that, Your Majesty— If they'll fit. *(He takes out his 18-inch ruler and holds it against the front of the box, counting off the inches, mumbling.)* There's ten and twelve—fourteen, sixteen, eighteen!

KING COLE. *(Anxiously.)* Is it big enough?

GROG. Well, now— *(He tries measuring from the other end.)* There's twelve and some more—and a bit of a line, and— Well! No question about *that!* *(Facing the* OTHERS.) It's more than eighteen inches, either way! *(He turns to* NICK *and tests the ruler against one of the fiddles.)* —And so are the fiddles!

QUEEN. But how much more?

GROG. That's hard to say, Your Majesty. The ruler isn't long enough. But if the box "more" is more than the fiddle "more"—or the other way around— That is, if the fiddle "more" is *not* more than the box "more"— *(He stops, scowling at the ruler.)* It's rather difficult.

NICK. Couldn't we just try them, sir? If they go in— well, then it's big enough, isn't it?

KING COLE. Of course! And if they don't go in, why, then it's *not* big enough! An excellent idea, Nick!

GROG. Well, it's not very scientific, Your Majesty, but— Yes, I suppose we *could* try them. We could do that. *(He puts away the ruler.)* If you'll give them to me—

> (NICK *hands him one after the other and he puts them into the box.)*

That's it— One—two—and three!

QUEEN. Do they fit?

GROG. *(Peering in at the fiddles.)* They do, Your Majesty. They fit as a fiddle—or as three fiddles, I should say. They fit very nicely. *(He reaches in to take them out again.)*

KING COLE. Splendid! You see, it *is* a good box for putting things in!

GROG. So it is, Your Majesty, but— Ha!—Yes, I— Hm!—I'm afraid it's *not* a very good box for taking things out!

KING COLE. How's that?

(The OTHERS *close in to peer uncertainly into the box. The* FIDDLERS *become more and more agitated as things progress.)*

GROG. They won't come out, Your Majesty!

*(NICK *joins him and they tug industriously.)*

QUEEN. Good heavens!

*(PENELOPE *goes to her.)*

Grog. The fact is, they're stuck!

King Cole. *(Peering into the box.)* By jingo!

Amelia. *(Excitedly.)* Maybe it's enchanted!

Celia. Oh, maybe it *is!*

Arabella. *(Almost at the same time.)* Maybe it's a *magic* box!

Tic, Tac, Toe. Terrible! *(They sing excitedly.)*
>   It's a dreadful situation,
>   It's a frightful complication,
>   It's a very sorry sort of mess!

(Grog straightens up abruptly, very nearly upsetting
Nick and the King.)

Grog. Silence!—Just so. If the fiddles are stuck—and they are—then we'll simply get them unstuck. It's nothing to get excited about.

King Cole. Are you sure?

Grog. Of course, Your Majesty. A bit of glue, most likely. A bit of glue in the bottom of the box. You can't very well set fiddles in glue and *not* have them stick. No, you can't very well do that!

Queen. But what *can* we do?

Grog. *(Considers.)* Well— We can melt the glue, of course. That's the easiest thing. It shouldn't take a very *big* fire.

Mrs. Smedly. Fire! In the throne room?

Grog. Just a small one, Mrs. Smedly.

Mrs. Smedly. I should say not! I'm the one who has to clean up in here!

Grog. Oh, very well— Boiling water will do just as well, I suppose. We can pour it in on top, and—

Tic, Tac, Toe. On the fiddles? !

Grog. Well, yes, it *would* get on the fiddles, of course—

Tic, Tac, Toe. Horrible!

(They are about to sing again, but the King intervenes,
cutting them off.)

KING COLE. Oh, we can't do that! We don't want *boiled* fiddles! Isn't there something else?

GROG. Possibly— Yes, there must be something, Your Majesty— *(As he thinks of it.)* So!—Bring me the glass!
    (NICK runs off up Left to get it.)
And open a window!—A high one, I think— That one up there!

(The FIDDLERS look where he points, Left, hesitate uncertainly, and then go to the side of the stage where a "'window rope" hangs from above. GROG studies the box, figuring the angle from the window.)

KING COLE. But— What are you going to do?

GROG. The sun, Your Majesty! We will melt the glue with the heat of the sun! Very simple!
    (NICK re-enters with a huge magnifying glass.)
Just so!—Here we are— Over here, Nick— That's the way—

QUEEN. Goodness!

(EVERYONE stands watching as GROG and NICK adjust the glass. A shaft of sunlight strikes from above, hitting the box. The FIDDLERS tie off the rope and stand by.)

GROG. *(Helping NICK with the magnifying glass.)* That's it, that's it!—We focus the sunlight into the box— A little higher, I think— So! *(To the KING, cheerfully.)* It won't take long, Your Majesty— I shouldn't think so—

(As EVERYONE watches, the sunbeam begins to fade while the box begins to glow.)

MRS. SMEDLY. Good heavens!

AMELIA. The box! It's—it's soaking up the sunlight!

CELIA. It is, it is!

GROG. What's that? !

ARABELLA. It *is* magic! It's soaking up the sun!

KING COLE. Goodness!

QUEEN. Stop it, someone! *Stop* it!

GROG. *(Excited, dropping the magnifying glass.)* Close the box! Close it, I say! Close it!

(The FIDDLERS, NICK *and* GROG *all rush to the box. After considerable confusion, they manage to close the lid —but the sun is already trapped, glowing brightly from inside the box.)*

PENELOPE. What is it?—What's happening?

MRS. SMEDLY. It's Crunch, that's what it is! And it's terrible!

QUEEN. But we can't have the sun in a box! Oh, dear, oh, dear! What will we *do?*

KING COLE. Open it, by jingo! That's the first thing! Open it up again!

NICK. Yes, sir!
   (He and GROG *try the lid.)*
Ouch!—It's getting hot, Your Majesty!

GROG. And it won't open! What's more— *(Abruptly, peering at the lid.)* Your Majesty! There's—there's something written here!

KING COLE. There is?

GROG. *(Reads.)*
   Here's a wondrous magic box!
   Oh, here's a box to think about:
   For when it shuts, it always locks;
   And what goes in will not come out!
   Here's a wondrous magic thing!
   Oh, here's a charm that cannot miss.
   To break the spell, you have to sing
   A magic song that goes like this!

KING COLE. Well, go on! Like what?

GROG. It—it doesn't say, Your Majesty— It just— stops!

NICK. *(Speaking for them all.)* Golly, Your Majesty!

KING COLE. By jingo!

THE CURTAIN FALLS

ACT TWO

THE SCENE: *The same, a few weeks later. The sun is still in the box. Several lanterns burn brightly, adding to the light in the room.*

(OVERTURE.)

AT RISE: KING COLE *sits upon his throne, blowing bubbles with his bubbles pipe. He is deep in thought. Nearby,* GROG *is shuffling through a handful of music, scowling and muttering to himself.* TIC, TAC *and* TOE *sit on the floor, sorting through a tremendous mound of songbooks, music, old papers, etc.* NICK *is standing, singing wearily to no audience.*

NICK. *(Singing without enthusiasm.)*
> The sunbeams dance a merry jig,
> The world is not so very big:
> It will fit in your hand,
> It's a magical land
> When you're singing—

(He breaks off, staring at the box.) It's no use, sir.

GROG. Try something else.

NICK. I don't think I know any more—

KING COLE. *(Jumping up.)* By jingo! *(Sings.)*
> "Rock-a-by baby, in the tree-top—"

GROG. No, Your Majesty. We've already tried it.

KING COLE. Are you sure?

NICK. Last week, sir. We tried it several times.

KING COLE. *(Sitting down again.)* Well—perhaps not, then—

GROG. *(Throwing away the music he holds.)* The fact is, Your Majesty, we've tried every kind of song we can find: quick, slow, long, short, high, low and in between! It's a terrible-thing-and-I'm-very-sorry, but none of them will open the box!

43

KING COLE. But there must be something!

GROG. Quite so. But what, where and how soon—that's something else again— It's a very gloomy sort of business.

KING COLE. Well, it's *bound* to be gloomy, of course, without any sun.

TIC, TAC, TOE. *(Pausing briefly for the line.)* And no fiddles!

GROG. Yes, we mustn't forget *that! (Counting it out on his fingers.)* No song, no sun; no sun, no fiddles; no fiddles, no party!

KING COLE. Goodness!

GROG. *(Becoming more and more excited.)* Badness, Your Majesty! That's what you mean to say. It's a very bad thing any way you look at it. And the way *I* look at it, it's even worse!—As Royal Regulator, it's impossible! I can't very well regulate things when I don't know whether it's night or day! And as Royal Jester, it's not funny! As Royal Magician, it's over my head, and as Royal *Physician*— *(He stops briefly to take his own temperature. He shows the thermometer to the* KING.*)* You see? It's *unhealthy!*

KING COLE. Well, it's *not* much fun—

GROG. *(Puts the thermometer away.)* And as Prime Minister, I suggest we *do* something!

KING COLE. Splendid!—Only—what shall we do?

GROG. That's the problem—

(They think a moment.)

KING COLE. A reward, do you think?

GROG. We've already done that, Your Majesty— *(He takes out a copy of the proclamation.)*

KING COLE. But a bigger one! Couldn't we offer a bigger reward?

GROG. I shouldn't think so— *(Reads.)* "By order of His Merry Majesty, King Cole of the Kingdom of Haw, any person who can find a way to open the magic box will be given his heart's desire."

KING COLE. Is that what it says?

GROG. His heart's desire, Your Majesty—

KING COLE. By jingo! I'd forgotten about that part! *(To* NICK.) Isn't that nice?

NICK. Yes, sir. But if no one can do it—

GROG. Exactly! *(He throws away the proclamation and takes out his memo book, finding the page he wants.)* It's not the reward so much, it's the people!—Sixty-eight people tried it the first week, Your Majesty; one hundred and seventy-two the second week; and last week—fifty-six!—As you can see, that's— Well, it's fifty-six and sixty-eight, plus one-seven-two. It's a *lot* of people, Your Majesty! It's very nearly all the people in the kingdom! *(He rips the page from the memo book and throws it away.)*

KING COLE. My goodness!

GROG. So it's not only a matter of what, where and how soon, it's also a matter of *who!* The trouble is, we're running out of people. And if there's no one left who can even *try* to open the box—

NICK. Golly, sir!

GROG. That's exactly what I mean!

TIC, TAC, TOE. Your Majesty! *(They scramble to their feet, pulling and tugging at a single sheet of music.)*

KING COLE. Good heavens!

GROG. Ho!—So!—Easy, now!—*Order!*

(The FIDDLERS *come to attention.)*
Well, now— One at a time!

TAC. *(Steps forward, followed by* TIC *and* TOE.) Your Majesty!

(They ALL *bow and come up singing furiously.)*

Song: *"Here's a Tune We Never Heard Of"*
TIC, TAC, TOE.   *(MUSIC CUE #9.)*
    Here's a tune we've never heard of,
    Never ever heard a word of,
    Here's a tune we've never heard before!
    It's a tune that's rather jolly,
    Very tra-la-la-la-lolly,
    It's a tune we really can't ignore!

TIC. *(Sings.)*
> It was underneath the others!

TAC. *(Sings.)*
> Underneath a stack of others!

TOE. *(Sings.)*
> Underneath the others on the floor!

TIC, TAC, TOE. *(Sing together.)*
> It could be a composition,
> By a wizard or magician:
> It could be the tune we're looking for!

KING COLE. By jingo!

GROG. *(Snatching the music from them.)* Magic, you say? The magic song?

KING COLE. A *new* song?

GROG. Just so!—It's a very strange bit of music, Your Majesty. I can't say it's *magic* music— No, I can't very well say that— But it does look that way. Quite possibly, it *is* the magic song!

KING COLE. Then try it! Try it!—Oh, good heavens yes!

TIC, TAC, TOE. Now?

GROG. Exactly! *(He gives them the music and herds them into position near the box, NICK helping.)* Over here, I think— Ready, now— Steady, now— Eyes on the box!

> (EVERYONE *looks hard at the box. The* KING *puts on a pair of dark glasses.*)

So! *(Using his magician's wand as a baton.)* One-two-three, ready go!

TIC, TAC, TOE. *(Singing.)* (*MUSIC CUE #10.*)
> Tra—la-la, tra-la-la, tra-la-la-la-la—

GROG. No, no, no, no! You can't be tra-la-la-ing all the way! You have to sing it! Sing the words! *(Raises the wand, ready to begin again.)*

TIC, TAC, TOE. We can't!

KING COLE. But why not?

TIC, TAC, TOE. Your Majesty—
> Song: "It's a Dreadful Situation"
> (*MUSIC CUE #11.*)

It's a dreadful situation,
It's a frightful complication,
It's a very sorry sort of mess!
All the words are wiggly wiggles,
Little bumps and lots of jiggles!
We don't know the meaning, we confess!

GROG. *(Snatching the music from them.)* What's this?

TIC. *(Sings.)*
It's a thing we've never heard of!

TAC. *(Sings.)*
We can't sing a single word of.

TOE. *(Sings.)*
We can't sing a single word of it!

GROG. Well!—Greek, Your Majesty. It's Greek to *me* at any rate. Or possibly Latin. No question about *that!*

KING COLE. Good heavens!

NICK. *(Looking over* GROG's *shoulder.)* But— Golly, sir! It's upside down, isn't it?

GROG. So!!!? *(He twists his head to look, keeping the music as it is. The* FIDDLERS *do the same.)* Well, now!— That *should* make a difference— *(He turns the music around and gives it back to the* FIDDLERS.) Now, then! *(He gives them the up-beat.)*

TIC, TAC, TOE. *(Singing.)*
"Rock-a-bye baby, in the tree-top—?"

(They stop uncertainly, staring at the music. GROG *throws away his wand and sits down abruptly, disgusted. The* FIDDLERS *throw away the music and trudge back to their sorting.)*

NICK. Golly, sir, it—it *did* make a difference!

KING COLE. *(Taking off his dark glasses; unhappily.)* But we've already tried that one!

GROG. And there's no magic in it, Your Majesty. No magic at all! I'm quite upset.

KING COLE. Goodness! At this rate, we never will find a song.

GROG. *(Gloomily.)* No song, no sun—

TIC, TAC, TOE. *(Mournfully.)* No fiddles!

NICK. And no party.

KING COLE. It's *not* very cheerful.

MRS. SMEDLY. *(Enters down Right, obviously excited.)* Your Majesty!

KING COLE. *(Unhappily.)* What is it, Mrs. Smedly?

MRS. SMEDLY. At the kitchen door, Your Majesty! People!

GROG. People, you say?

MRS. SMEDLY. A man and his wife! And they say they can open the box!

KING COLE. They do?

GROG. *(Jumps up, ready for business.)* Well, now!

KING COLE. Show them in, by jingo! Show them in!

GROG. But not just yet, Your Majesty, not at all! If they *can* open the box, they'll want the reward. And if we're going to give a reward, we have to do it properly. *And* officially! It's in the Regulations!

KING COLE. That's true, of course—

MRS. SMEDLY. And just look at this room! *(To the* FIDDLERS.*)* Pick it up, pick it up, now!—Goodness! *(She starts off, calling as she goes.)* Amelia! Celia! Arabell-*a? (She exits up Left.)*

(There is a great flurry of activity as the FIDDLERS *start picking up music.* NICK *joins them.)*

GROG. *(To no one in particular.)* Assemble the court! —Call the Queen!—Get *ready!*— *(He stops abruptly.)* Oh, bother!

KING COLE. What is it?

GROG. The scepter, Your Majesty! We have to have that! *(He rushes off up Left to get it.)*

KING COLE. And the Queen!—Yes, indeed! *(He rushes off in the opposite direction up Center.)*

(In the process of cleaning up, NICK *finds* GROG's *magic wand. He tucks it into his belt, picks up a stack of music and starts off up Left. He comes face to face with* PENELOPE.*)*

PENELOPE. *(Entering; excited.)* Is it true? Is someone really going to open the box?

NICK. *(Embarrassed.)* I— Well, I—I guess— Your Highness.

PENELOPE. *(Stares at him.)* What?

> (NICK *tries to bow—an awkward business, because of the music.* PENELOPE *takes his arm and straightens him up.*)

Oh, don't do that!—My goodness!

NICK. As you wish, Your Highness.

PENELOPE. What's the matter with you?

> (NICK'S *answer is to stand even more rigidly.* PENELOPE *is forced to dodge the* FIDDLERS *as they go back and forth, carrying music off-stage throughout the conversation.*)

Nick?

NICK. Yes'm?

PENELOPE. We *are* friends, aren't we?

NICK. *(Terribly uncomfortable.)* As you wish, Your Highness.

PENELOPE. Oh, stop it! It's no fun at all if you're going to be like that! Don't you *want* to be friends?

NICK. Well, I—I mean— You're a *Princess!*

PENELOPE. There's nothing wrong with that, is there?

NICK. *(Painfully.)* Yes'm.

PENELOPE. Oh!—Well, I—I can't help what you think. But I'd much rather be a Princess than a—a snob! *(She turns away.)*

NICK. But—!

(One of the FIDDLERS *bumps him from behind. The impact sends him stumbling off up Left with his load of music. At the same time,* MRS. SMEDLY *re-enters with the* LADIES-IN-WAITING. *A moment later, the* KING *enters up Center with the* QUEEN.)*

MRS. SMEDLY. Come along, now, we haven't a moment! —Pick it up, pick it up!—That's the way!

(The LADIES-IN-WAITING *gather up what remains of the music and exit with it up Left.)*

KING COLE. *(Entering, almost at the same time.)* Hurry, m'love!—Hurry, now!—They're just outside—

QUEEN. *(As they scurry to the throne.)* What a wonderful thing! I can hardly believe it! Just think if they *can* open the box! *(Sees* PENELOPE.) Come, dear. Take your place, now!

(PENELOPE *joins them, standing beside the throne.* NICK *re-enters. The* FIDDLERS *line up on one side of the stage, as* GROG *comes rushing in with the scepter.)*

GROG. Steady, now! Ready, now!—Ho! *(He comes to a stop and looks around.)* Is everyone here?

(The LADIES-IN-WAITING *scurry on-stage and take their places near* MRS. SMEDLY.)*

MRS. SMEDLY. Of course we are!

KING COLE. Can't we begin?

GROG. Just so! *(He raps with the scepter.)* All hail to His Merry Majesty! King Cole, Ruler of the Kingdom of—

KING COLE. Oh, never mind all that! Get to the man and his wife!

GROG. In a moment, Your Majesty. First, we have to do the singing.

KING COLE. But can't we do it later?

GROG. I shouldn't think so. Not according to the Regulations.

KING COLE. Oh, very well, then, but *quickly!*

GROG. *Very* quickly, Your Majesty! *(Raps with the scepter; rapidly.)* Make-way-I-say-for-the-king!

                 (MUSIC CUE #12.)

ALL. *(Singing as rapidly as possible.)*
  Make way for the king,
  Make way for the king,
  He's all that a king should be!
  Make way for the king,

    Make way for the king,
    Make way for His Majesty!
        La-dee-da-dee-da-dee-da,
        La-dee-da-dee-da-dee-da,
        La-dee-da-dee-da-dee-da-dee-da-dee-da-dum!
    Make way for the king,
    Hooray for the king,
    Hooray for Old King Cole!

KING COLE. Splendid! Now, where are they!?

GROG. Who, Your Majesty?

KING COLE. Why, the *people!* The ones who say they can open the box!

GROG. Oh, of course! *(He raps with the scepter.)* All those having·business with the King will now step forward!

(BLACK and LOCK SMITH enter tentatively down Right. BLACK is a burly fellow, wearing a blacksmith's apron and a tool-pouch. His wife is smaller, with keys dangling from the brim of her hat. She wears an enormous hat-pin.)

BLACK. Us?

GROG. Exactly. Come along, now— So!—Your name?

BLACK. Smith, sir. Black Smith. This is my wife, Lock.

GROG. *(Banging the scepter.)* If it please the court, Mr. and Mrs. Smith! *(He ushers them towards the throne.)*

(They shuffle forward and bob their heads at the KING and QUEEN.)

KING COLE. Well, now!

BLACK. 'Morning, Your Majesty.

LOCK. Or evening, sir, whichever it is—

BLACK. We'd like to try the box.

KING COLE. Splendid! Do you hear that, my dear? They want to try it!

QUEEN. Yes, but—everyone's *tried*— *(To the SMITHS.)* Do you know the magic song?

BLACK. Oh, no, ma'am!

LOCK. We don't know any magic, ma'am.

BLACK. But what we *do* know is boxes!

KING COLE. *Magic* boxes?

BLACK. Any kind, sir. We've never seen a box we couldn't open.

LOCK. Nary a one, sir. All it takes is a pick or a bang!

QUEEN. Dear!

BLACK. What she means, ma'am, if she can't pick the lock, then I just bang the hinges off.

KING COLE. By jingo!—But don't you need tools?

BLACK. We brought the tools, sir. *(He takes a hammer and cold chisel from his tool-pouch.)*

LOCK. *(Pulling out her hat-pin.)* We never go out without 'em!

BLACK. So all we need is the box.

KING COLE. Well, it's—it's right over there.

(The SMITHS go to the box, looking it over. The members of the court watch anxiously. The KING puts on his dark glasses.)

LOCK. *(To BLACK.)* What do you think?

BLACK. *(Shrugs.)* Ladies first, I guess.

LOCK. Good! *(She starts probing with the hat-pin, hesitates, and tries again, gradually working her way completely around the box.)*

KING COLE. *(To the QUEEN.)* Is she doing it?

QUEEN. I can't tell.

PENELOPE. It looks like she's looking!

LOCK. *(Completing her tour.)* Funny!—There's no lock!

BLACK. Are you sure?

LOCK. No lock at all! I've never seen such a box!

BLACK. Well, it *has* to have hinges. Even a magic box has those! *(He goes behind the box with his tools.)* Ah-ha!—We'll open it now, all right! *(He bangs away.)*

(EVERYONE backs up nervously.)

QUEEN. *(Covering her ears.)* Goodness!

BLACK. *(Stops banging abruptly.)* Oh!

KING COLE. Well?—What is it?

BLACK. *(Dismayed.)* It's—it's *hot,* Your Majesty!

GROG. Oh, of course it's hot! We've got the sun in there !

BLACK. But—my chisel! It's melted my chisel! *(He holds it up, and sure enough! There is general consternation.)*

KING COLE. *(Snatching off the dark glasses.)* Melted, you say?

BLACK. *(Wailing.)* My very best chisel! *(Sobbing, he lurches off stage down Right.)*

LOCK. *(Pausing on her way out.)* It was, too, Your Majesty! The very best chisel he ever had! *(She exits after* BLACK.*)*

KING COLE. *(Jumping up.)* But wait a minute!

GROG. It's no use, Your Majesty. They've gone.

QUEEN. Oh, and there *won't* be anyone else! I just know it!

GROG. *(Glumly.)* Well, it's not likely. Everyone's tried it— No people, no song, no sun, no fiddles—

QUEEN. But what will we *do?!*

KING COLE. *(Sitting down again; hopelessly.)* Exactly, my dear— What *will* we do?

(General despondency. PENELOPE *bursts into tears, burying her head in the* QUEEN's *lap.* NICK *starts towards her, checks himself, and turns to* GROG.*)*

NICK. Oh, golly, sir— There *must* be something!

GROG. You'd think so. But the fact is, there's nothing. Nothing at all.

NICK. But we can't just give up! Maybe there *is* a song! Just because we don't know it *now* doesn't mean we never will. I know lots of songs I didn't used to know!

GROG. But not the *right* one. That's the trouble, you see.

NICK. Well, look, sir—pretend there *is* a song. Pretend

there's a—a magician or something *outside* the kingdom.
If he knew the song he'd tell us, wouldn't he? He'd come
right up to the castle and claim the reward! We'd know
then, wouldn't we?

GROG. Just so! But that's pretending, Nick. It's not the
same as happening, I should think.

NICK. But it *could* happen!

*(And BANG, it does. The back doors of the house open
and a MESSENGER runs pell-mell down the aisle to
the stage. GROG looks at NICK, who shrugs helplessly. EVERYONE moves down to meet the MESSENGER.
PENELOPE stops crying, and the KING and QUEEN
stand up for a better look.)*

MESSENGER. *(Running down the aisle.)* Your Majesty!
Your Majesty!

KING COLE. Good heavens!

QUEEN. What *is* it?

MESSENGER. *(Arrives on stage, gasping.)* Your Majesty—!

GROG. *(As he and NICK support the MESSENGER.)* Ho!
—So!—Easy, now!

NICK. Are you all right?

MESSENGER. Out of breath, is all— I ran all the way—

KING COLE. Goodness!

MESSENGER. From the edge of the kingdom, Your
Majesty— He's coming!

GROG. He?

KING COLE. *Who?*

MESSENGER. Well, I don't know *who*, exactly, but he
says he's a great magician! And he's coming to claim the
reward!

GROG. Oh, but he can't do that! He can't just claim it,
he has to open the box!

MESSENGER. He will, sir. He *says* he will— He knows
the magic song!

GROG. Are you sure?

MESSENGER. That's what he says, sir.

KING COLE. By jingo!

NICK. *(Pointing into the house.)* Your Majesty!

MESSENGER. It's him!

QUEEN. *(Flustered and excited.)* Oh, dear, oh, dear, oh, *dear!*

(EVERYONE *crowds forward to watch as* CRUNCH *comes down the aisle, mumbling, chuckling to himself. He wears a cloak and carries a suitcase. A muffler hides most of his face.)*

KING COLE. We'd better sit down, m'love!

(They hurry back to the throne.)

GROG. *(Watching* CRUNCH'S *progress.)* Ready, now—Steady, now!—And mind your manners!

KING COLE. Oh, yes, indeed! We *don't* want to make him angry!

GROG. Just so! *(He moves to the top of the "drawbridge" as* CRUNCH *arrives at the foot of it. He bows rather stiffly.)* We have heard of your coming, good sir. Enter and welcome, both officially and otherwise.

(CRUNCH *gives a chuckley grunt and climbs to the stage. As he does so,* GROG *motions to the* FIDDLERS.)

Quick, now!—Luggage and cloak, and careful-of-his-hat!

(The FIDDLERS *rush forward. One of them takes the suitcase; another the hat. The third stands by to help with the cloak.)*

(GROG *turns to the throne, hesitates, and then looks at* CRUNCH *again, uncertainly.)* You *are* the gentleman we've heard of, I suppose?

(CRUNCH *mutters into his muffler.)*

A great magician?

(CRUNCH *inclines his head, a half-bow of acknowledgement, as he slips out of his cloak.)*

Well, then!

(As he turns to the throne, CRUNCH *begins to unwind the muffler.)*

(GROG *raps with the scepter.*) If it please the court, one great magician, a stranger—

KING COLE. (*Jumping up, staring at* CRUNCH.) Good heavens!

MRS. SMEDLY. (*At almost the same time.*) It's Crunch!

(*There is a general reaction. The* FIDDLERS *drop hat, suitcase and cloak and jump away.*)

GROG. (*Whirling about.*) Ho?—So!—It *is* Crunch!

CRUNCH. (*Walks forward, immensely pleased with himself. He bows to the throne.*) I have returned, Your Majesty—

GROG. (*Excited.*) But look here! You can't do that! You've been banished!

KING COLE. That's true! It's no good banishing people if they come right back again!

CRUNCH. That's technical, Your Majesty. I won't argue about that. The point is, I've come to open the box.

KING COLE. You have?

QUEEN. You mean you *are* a great magician?

CRUNCH. (*Bows to her.*) Your Majesty—

(*MUSIC CUE #13.*)

Song: "I'm a Great Magicianer"

I know the secret history
Of ev'ry kind of mystery;
I know the what and whichery
Of magic and of witchery!
    So just look out
    When I'm about!
I'm a great magician, yes, I am!

(*He prowls about, chuckling and growling.*) I told you so!—Oh, I knew you'd be sorry! (*Sings.*)

'Cause I'm a great magicianer,
A super superstitioner,
A magic exhibitioner,
A hobble-gobble-itioner!
    And you'll find out
    When I'm about!
I'm a great magician, yes, I am!

KING COLE. *(Uncomfortably.)* Well, of course—in that case—

QUEEN. And if you *can* open the box—

KING COLE. We could never mind about the banishment, I suppose. Temporarily, at least.

GROG. Well, I hardly think so, Your Majesty. It's *not* a proper way of doing things. Except for him, there wouldn't *be* a banishment! And no box! No box, no banishment. Except for him, it wouldn't have happened.

QUEEN. But it *did* happen!

KING COLE. And if he's ready to make it right again—!

GROG. Well— There *is* that, I suppose. And we *should* get the box open—

KING COLE. Exactly! *(To* CRUNCH.) Crunch, you are hereby and forthwith *un*banished—at least temporarily, and we-shall-see!—That means you have to open the box.

CRUNCH. Thank you, Your Majesty. But before I do, there's something else.

KING COLE. There is?

CRUNCH. The reward, Your Majesty.

GROG. Oh, now, really! You can't have a reward for something that's your fault. It's not fair!

KING COLE. And I've already changed the banishment!

CRUNCH. That's your business. I'll have to have the reward, I think. No reward, no song.

GROG. *(Unhappily.)* No song, no sun, Your Majesty—

QUEEN. Goodness!

KING COLE. Well, that does make a difference, of course— What is it you want?

CRUNCH. *(Chuckling.)* No more than you offered, Your Majesty. My heart's desire!

KING COLE. Your—your heart's desire?

GROG. *(Unhappily.)* That *is* the reward, Your Majesty.

KING COLE. But— Good heavens! That could be anything!

GROG. It *could,* but the fact is, it can't! I shouldn't think so. The point is, he has to ask for something we have. We can't very well give him *anything,* Your Majesty. It has to be *something!*

CRUNCH. *(Chuckling diabolically.)* Oh, it is, it is! Indeed, it is!

KING COLE. Money?

GROG. *(To* CRUNCH.) We *do* have that, you know. Thirty-seven cents, left over from buying the new fiddles. If you'd like that—

QUEEN. Or a place at court—

KING COLE. By jingo!—You *did* ask to be Court Magician!

CRUNCH. But that was some time ago, Your Majesty. I've changed my mind.

GROG. Then what *do* you want?

CRUNCH. *(Bows mockingly.)* If it please the court—a crown.

(There is general consternation. The KING *raises his hands to his crown uncertainly.)*

KING COLE. A—a crown, you say? But if I gave you the *crown—!*

CRUNCH. Then *I'd* be king!

GROG. Ho!
MRS. SMEDLY. Nonsense!
FIDDLERS. Awful!!
QUEEN. Oh, *dear!*   } *(Simultaneously.)*
PENELOPE. King?!
LADIES-IN-WAITING. Oh, no!
NICK. Golly!

CRUNCH. Oh, you'd like me *then,* I guess! You'd have to! *(He stamps his foot at them and turns back to the* KING; *unctuously.)* Shall I open the box, sir?

PENELOPE. Oh, no!

ALL. *(Ad lib.)* Oh, no, Your Majesty! No! No! No!

QUEEN. You just *can't* give him the crown!

KING COLE. *(Unhappily.)* Well, I—I don't like to, of course— I'm rather fond of being king— But it's not just me, my dear. *Everybody* needs the sun, I should think.

CRUNCH. Is it a bargain, then?

KING COLE. I guess it *has* to be. *(He sits down heavily.)*
(The QUEEN *bursts into tears.* CRUNCH *clicks his
heels and trots happily over to the box.)*

There, there, my dear. He's just doing it out of spite. And
we *will* have the sun again.

CRUNCH. *(At the box; gleefully.)* A king, a king, I'll
be a king! And all I have to do is sing! *(Chuckling and
rubbing his hands.)* Oh, it's magic, is it?—Then listen to
this! *(He strikes a pose and recites.)*

(MUSIC CUE #14.)

> Here's a wondrous magic box!
> Oh, here's a box to think about!
> For when it shuts, it always locks;
> And what goes in will not come out!
> Here's a wondrous magic thing!
> Oh, here's a charm that cannot miss!
> To break the spell, you have to sing
> A magic song that goes like this:

(He stops, puzzled, and then repeats:)

> To break the spell, you have to sing—

(His self-assurance rapidly disintegrates.) You have to
sing—!!!?

GROG. So?

CRUNCH. I—I've forgotten!

KING COLE. By jingo!

GROG. Forgotten, you say?

*(His tone of voice is echoed in the murmur of indigna-
tion that comes from the* OTHERS. CRUNCH *nods
fearfully, easing away from the box.)*

KING COLE. You mean you *can't* open the box?

*(*CRUNCH *makes a break for it. There is general whoop-
ing and hooting and squeals from the* LADIES.*)*

GROG. Ho! Ho, I say!—Stop him, stop him!

(The FIDDLERS *block* CRUNCH'S *escape at one side of the
stage; he reverses his field and is collared by* NICK.*)*

NICK. Got him, sir!

(CRUNCH *makes a half-hearted effort to break away, gives up, and stands helplessly, his power gone.*)

GROG. Well, now! *(He hesitates, then abruptly consults the Book of Regulations.)*

KING COLE. Well?

QUEEN. What do we do *now?*

GROG. It's hard to say, Your Majesty— It's *not* in the Regulations, you see—nothing about boxes and running away. But if I may say so, he *did* make a bargain, and a bargain ought to be kept!

KING COLE. That's true, of course—

CRUNCH. But I can't!

GROG. In that case, there *is* no bargain. No song, no crown! No song, no sun, and all the rest of it! We're right back where we started. And *I* say he ought to be banished again!

CRUNCH. *(Suddenly smitten with the truth.)* Your Majesty—?

KING COLE. Yes?

CRUNCH. There's—there's no sun!

GROG. Of course there's no sun! And it's your fault!

CRUNCH. But if I can't remember—there won't *be* any sun! Never! And when you look at it that way, it's—it's kind of scary! *(There is an uneasy murmur of agreement.)* I've done a terrible thing!

KING COLE. And you *should* be ashamed of yourself!

CRUNCH. Oh, I am!—I am!   *(MUSIC CUE #15.)*
        Song: *"I'm a Wicked Rascal, Yes, I Am"*
            I'm so ashamed, Your Majesty,
            It's only just occured to me,
            I've acted very wickedly,
            So wicked in my trickery!
                Oh, what a mess!
                I must confess,
            I'm a wicked rascal, yes, I am!

KING COLE. Well, you *haven't* been very nice.

GROG. The fact is, you've been *bad!*

CRUNCH. And *that's* why nobody likes me!—I'm *mean!*

GROG. Exactly!

CRUNCH. There's—there's nothing I can do, I suppose —to make up for it. If I could *do* something—

KING COLE. There's nothing much, I'm afraid— Except the box—

QUEEN. Oh, yes! Oh, *dear*, yes!

GROG. You *could* remember how to do it. Open the box, I mean. It's not much to ask, I should think, all things considered.

CRUNCH. *(Sadly, shaking his head.)* But— Oh! *(He brightens suddenly.)* I do! I do! I remember!

(EVERYONE *reacts.*)

KING COLE. The magic song?

CRUNCH. *(Excited.)* I *knew* I might forget, so I *did* something to remind myself!

KING COLE. Splendid!

GROG. What was it?

CRUNCH. *(Uncertainly.)* Well, I—I don't remember that part—

MRS. SMEDLY. *(As* EVERYONE *reacts.)* Nonsense!

NICK. Was it a *thing?*

GROG. You wrote it down!

CRUNCH. No, I—I don't think I wrote it down.

KING COLE. Where would it be?

QUEEN. Oh, *do* try to remember!

CRUNCH. Well—my—my suitcase, possibly, or—

TIC, TAC, TOE. Suitcase!

(They grab the suitcase and put it on a chair. They open it and start throwing things out right and left: shirts, socks, a ball of string, a large tooth-brush, a yo-yo, etc. MRS. SMEDLY, *the* LADIES-IN-WAITING, NICK *and the* FIDDLERS *begin grabbing things and holding them up to* CRUNCH *hopefully.)*

ALL. *(Ad lib., as they try various articles.)* This?—Is it this?—Here's something! *(Etc.)*

CRUNCH. *(A bit dazed by the onslaught.)* No— No—
I don't— No, that's not it— I don't think so.
GROG. Think, man, think!

*(EVERYONE stands about, waving whatever they hold
hopefully. NICK goes back to the suitcase and looks
inside.)*

CRUNCH. It—it must be something else.
KING COLE. But what?!
NICK. *(At the suitcase.)* There *isn't* anything else in
here—except these. *(He holds up two brightly colored
bottles.)*
GROG. Is *that* it?
CRUNCH. *(Considers as the OTHERS wait breathlessly.)*
Well—no. I know what that is. Hair tonic and shoe
polish—
QUEEN. *(Expressing the general disappointment.)*
Shoe polish!

*(EVERYONE turns away, depressed, throwing the contents
of the suitcase into a heap beside the chair. CRUNCH
is hard at work, mumbling, humming, trying to remember. NICK puts the bottles down. As he does so,
they clink together. The sound catches his ear. He
eyes them speculatively, then takes out GROG's magic
wand, still in his belt.)*

KING COLE. Well—if that's *all*—
GROG. There's no hope.
NICK. Listen! *(He hits one bottle and then the other
with the wand: a high and then a low tone.)*
CRUNCH. Oh, don't do that!—I'm trying to remember!
NICK. *(Hitting them again, delighted.)* But it's nice,
isn't it? *(He continues to strike the bottles, high-low,
high-low, making a rhythm.)*
CRUNCH. But how can I think? How can I— Ha?—So?
(He stops suddenly, listening.) That's it!
GROG. *(Voicing the general reaction.)* It?!

(CRUNCH *hops about, excited, as he starts to sing. The song develops as a round, as first* NICK, *then the* FIDDLERS, *then* PENELOPE *and the* LADIES-IN-WAITING, *and finally the* KING, QUEEN, GROG *and* MRS. SMEDLY *join in. Each group continues to sing the second "Magic! Magic!" until all are ready to sing the last line in unison.)   *(MUSIC CUE #16.)*

CRUNCH.
Magic! Magic!
Lolly-dolly-dolly-did!   (NICK *starts.*)
Magic! Magic!   (FIDDLERS *start.*)
Magic! Magic!   (PENELOPE, LADIES-IN-WAITING.)
Magic! Magic!   (KING, QUEEN, MRS. SMEDLY,
Magic! Magic!   GROG.)
Magic! Magic!   (ALL *in unison.*)
        ALL.
Open up the lid!
        (The lid of the box springs open—or is opened by NICK, *if necessary—and* SUNLIGHT *floods the room abruptly.)*
The sun! The sun!
        TIC, TAC, TOE. *(Getting them out of the box.)* The fiddles!
        PENELOPE. And we *will* have a party after all!
        ALL. *(Great rejoicing, ad lib.)* Hooray! Hoorah! *(Etc., etc.)*
        GROG. *(Rapping with the scepter.)* One thing at a time! *(As he gets their attention.)* We *still* have to give the reward, Your Majesty! It's in the Regulations!
        KING COLE. Of course! But—who do we give it to?
        GROG. Why, Nick, Your Majesty! He *did* find a way to open the box. *(Raps with the scepter.)* Young Nicholas of Nowhere!
        KING COLE. *(As* NICK *is pushed forward.)* Splendid! You do have a heart's desire, I suppose?
        NICK. *(Self-consciously.)* Well—yes, Your Majesty. But I can't ask for that, I guess—
        GROG. And why not?

NICK. Well, sir—and if it please the court—I am but an Apprentice Fool, and—and she's a Princess.

KING COLE. By jingo! *(To* PENELOPE.) What do you say to *that*, my dear?

PENELOPE. *(As she sings, she moves to* NICK, *who almost runs away in a panic but doesn't.)*

(MUSIC CUE #17.)

Song: "A Fool Would Be Wise"
A Fool would be wise if he knew
That a Princess can be foolish, too.
And if you turn away,
Nothing more to say,
Think how foolish I'll be,
Pretending you really are in love with me—

(NICK *points to himself in disbelief, asking with his eyebrows.* PENELOPE *nods self-consciously.)*

NICK. *(Overcome, but liking it.)* Golly! *(He takes her hand shyly.)*

KING COLE. And you *are* a prince of a fellow, Nick!—Now we *really* have something to celebrate!

CRUNCH. *(Abruptly.)* Your Majesty!

(There is silence as EVERYONE *looks at him, fearing a relapse into wickedness.)*

I—I just thought of something, Your Majesty!—It was going to be a coming-out party—for the King's *daughter*. But now it's a coming-out party for the *sun!*—Out of the box, you see? Sun? Daughter?—It's a *joke!* I made a joke!

(EVERYONE *laughs at and with* CRUNCH.)

KING COLE. By jingo, so you did! And you *will* have a crown after all! *(He removes* GROG's *hat, much to the latter's astonishment, and puts it on* CRUNCH's *head.)* There, now!

GROG. *(Horrified.)* But—Prime Minister?

KING COLE. Oh, no! Royal Jester! *(Putting his hand on top of the hat.)* Crunch, you have proved yourself a natural-born Fool!

(A jack-in-the-box Punch springs out from the top of the hat—or, more simply, the KING pulls out a concealed cloth extension that converts the hat to a Jester's cap.)

ALL. *(A tremendous cheer.)* Hooray!
                     (MUSIC CUE #18.)
(CRUNCH cuts a caper, bowing in turn to the KING, the QUEEN, MRS. SMEDLY and GROG as EVERYONE sings:)

           Song: "Pretend"

Pretend you're a king or a clown!
Either way, you'll be wearing a crown!
There's nothing to it,
You can do it,
Just you wait and see!
A clown or a king is what you'll be!

(TIC, TAC and TOE step forward, sawing on their one-string, Haw-type fiddles, while the LADIES-IN-WAITING dance.)

Pretend you can fiddle-diddle-dee!
Fiddle-lie, fiddle-lum, fiddle-lee!
There's nothing to it,
You can do it,
Just you wait and see!
A fee, fiddle-diddle-diddle-dee!

(To the audience, NICK and PENELOPE leading.)

Pretend and it's all up to you!
There's no end to the things you can do!
There's nothing to it,
You can do it,
Just you wait and see!
Pretending—you're anything you want to be!

THE CURTAIN FALLS.

OLD KING COLE

PROPERTY PLOT

Permanent Set:
2 thrones (Right)
Small table (between thrones)
Stool or low chair (down Right)
Bench or chairs (Left)
Large toy-chest, designed to hold lighting unit for "magic"
    box (up Center)
Rack or standard to hold scepter (beside King's throne)
Pull rope for "window" (hangs Left)

Act One, Scene I:
Large box filled with bright-colored papers (L.C.)
Length of silken material, needle and thread (Mrs. Smed-
    ly)
Princess' crown and sequins (Queen)
3 mops (Fiddlers)

(Grog)
Quiver or large holster containing:
    Magician's wand
    Jester's stick
    Doctor's thermometer (over-sized)
    18-inch ruler
Bubble pipe
Royal scepter
Calendar page
Memo book
Large pocket watch
Book of Royal Regulations
Royal Regulator's report
Royal Physician's report
A Plan of the Party

The King's Bowl (in the toy-chest and/or brought on
    by Amelia)

Vagabond's stick and bundle (Nick)
Bits and pieces of "fiddles," including a fiddle-head with
    string attached (Mrs. Smedly)
Large book (Grog)
Bulging carpet-bag with umbrella strapped to it (Crunch)
Large, ornate magic-box, translucent (Crunch)
Large tag (Crunch)
Handkerchief (Crunch)

Act One, Scene II:
A dozen or more paper party hats (Ladies-in-Waiting)
3 Haw-type, one-string fiddles (Nick)
Large "magnifying" glass (approximately 3 feet in di-
    ameter) (Nick)

Act Two:
Three or four lanterns (placed about the set)
A great quantity of songbooks, sheet music, old paper,
    etc. (on the floor Center)
Proclamation (Grog)
Dark glasses (King Cole)
Hat-pin (Lock)
Hammer and cold chisel (Black)
"Melted" cold chisel (Black)

(Crunch) {
    Suitcase, containing:
        Shirts, socks, woolen drawers, etc.
        Yo-yo
        Out-sized toothbrush
        Ball of string
        Two brightly colored bottles

IT'S A DREADFUL SITUATION!
HERE'S A TUNE WE NEVER HEARD OF!
CUES #3 - #4 - #9 - #10

PRETEND!
CUES #5 - #8 - #17

(NOTE: SEE NEXT PAGE FOR WALTZ VERSION)

PRETEND!
(WALTZ VERSION)
(A FOOL WOULD BE WISE)

I'M A GREAT MAGICIANER!
I'M A WICKED RASCAL, YES, I AM!
CUES #6-#13-#15

MAKE WAY FOR THE KING!
OVERTURE AND CUES #1-#12

SING A MERRY SONG!
CUE #2

MAGIC!
CUES #7 - #14

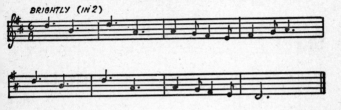

ROCK-A-BYE REVERSED!

NOTE: TRA-LA-LA-ED BY THE FIDDLERS WITHOUT ACCOMPANIMENT

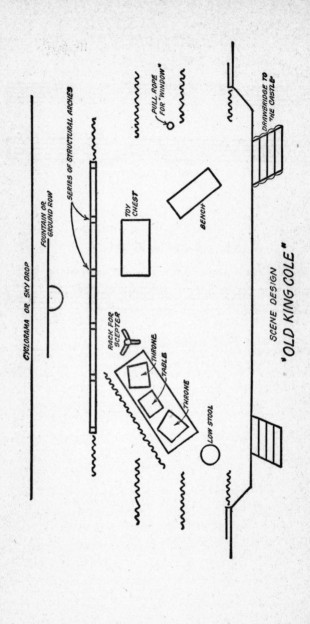

CYCLORAMA OR SKY DROP

FOUNTAIN OR GROUND ROW

SERIES OF STRUCTURAL ARCHES

PULL ROPE FOR "WINDOW"

TOY CHEST

BENCH

DRAWBRIDGE TO "THE CASTLE"

RACK FOR SCEPTER

THRONE

TABLE

THRONE

LOW STOOL

SCENE DESIGN
"OLD KING COLE"

CURTAIN GOING UP

Comedy. 3 acts. By Gregory Johnston. 7 men, 10 women. Extras. No scenery. Modern costumes.

Every once in a while a play by a new author is so entertaining that it is a pleasure to introduce his work. Such a comedy is *Curtain Going Up* by Gregory Johnston. It is the story, in comic terms, of the production of a play in a high school, and the action takes place on the stage and in the auditorium, during rehearsals and after the presentation. Among the myriad comic obstacles with which poor Miss Burgess is faced (it is her first play) are the following: a grouchy janitor with a sharp tongue, the disappearance of the playbooks the first day of rehearsal, a set of comically crossed-up high school romances with a capital R, a charming young heroine who becomes stagestruck, her bewildered boyfriend, a campus "actor" with a swollen head, the disgruntled athlete feeling out of place as an actor, a flamboyant professional actress with advice, a banker's daughter driven to theft and dirty tricks by her father's ambitions—and, perhaps most unexpected of all, a romance for young Miss Burgess herself!

(Royalty, $25.00.)

SKY HIGH

Comedy. 3 acts. By Florence Ryerson and Alice D. G. Miller. 9 men. 5 women. Interior. Modern costumes.

A gay and rollicking group of college students are marooned at Sky High, a skiing lodge, during the Christmas holidays, by the caving in of a tunnel. In the middle of their merry-making they discover the place is headquarters for a group of spies who are using it as a lookout and short-wave station. For ninety thrilling minutes the young people pull themselves out of one danger only to plunge into another. By the end of the evening the boy who feared he was a coward has learned he can be brave when danger threatens his girl; the bird-brained Toots has saved them by accident; while the absent-minded Mr. Mundy has proved himself a master-mind. The principal parts are equal in importance, the setting simple. A real treasure for the school or little theatre director who wants a fast-moving comedy with a slant as modern as tomorrow.

(Royalty, $25.00.)

Musical Productions Controlled by

Samuel French, Inc.

SEVENTEEN
THE MERRY WIDOW
WONDERFUL WALTZ
THE VAGABOND KING
THE DESERT SONG
THE CHOCOLATE SOLDIER
OF THEE I SING
GOOD NEWS
THREE TO ONE
THREE WISHES FOR JAMIE
THE GINGHAM GIRL
THE FIREMAN'S FLAME
OH! SUSANNA
NAUGHTY NAUGHT
THE GIRL FROM WYOMING
MY CHINA DOLL
ROSALIE RUNS RIOT
THE SWEETEST GIRL IN TOWN
LITTLE WOMEN
OUR NIGHT OUT
HARMONY HALL
THE BACHELOR BELLES
THE PRINCESS RUNS AWAY
GOLDEN DAYS
THE TALES OF HOFFMAN
OLD KING COLE

A descriptive list of "French's Musical **Library**"
will be sent on request